The Deep

CURT SIMMONS

Dedication

For the people of Friendship Church – who have been on this roller coaster ride of faith since the beginning.

Special thanks to Dawn, Suzie, Angela, and Tom.

Contents

Deep calls to deep in the roar of your waterfalls; all your waves and breakers have swept over me.

By day the Lord directs his love; at night his song is with me. A prayer to the God of my life.

PSALM 42: 7 & 8

It Felt Like Turbulence...

Except I wasn't moving.

It was a time when I felt like giving up. You know the feeling - when you can't get past the moment, or see past the situation. I had reached a place of desperation. If you've never felt that way, you will at some point.

I was riding an ATV, trying to relax – to clear my mind – to find a solution to an unsolvable problem. I stopped, turned off the ignition, and sat alone in the middle of the woods. I started talking to God. I told him everything – what I thought, how I felt, how angry I was – I told him stuff you're not supposed to tell God. I told him everything that was in my heart.

And that's when it happened. Like turbulence.

The woods were quiet, not a breath of wind – this was a turbulence of the soul. It came with a simple, calming thought in the middle of my personal storm: *Everything is going to be all right*. I had no reason to believe the thought, but I knew it was true. And I knew one single reality at that moment – God was very near. I felt like there was only an invisible wall between us. It was a moment that built my faith. A moment that made me believe with new eyes – to have hope in hopelessness.

Since that time, my faith has been deep... and shallow. I've been close to God... and sometimes, I've been far away. Sometimes there is a canyon between us that my sin and actions have created. Sometimes, the space between us seems so close that I could almost break through it.

For the believer, this is the walk of life – the space of faith. It's where *what you know* and *what you believe* are often challenged by God's Spirit and through his word. Faith – a narrow and difficult trail.

And yet, the Scripture says, *"Come close to God and God will come close to you."* (James 4:8). Isn't that what we want in the end? To just be near him?

But the journey of life that leads to eternity with him is full of ups and downs. It is full of steep inclines, rocky cliffs, deep valleys – and yes, mountaintop moments.

And it's all about faith.

I pray these pages help ease your ascent and that you find your faith *deep* along the way.

Part 1

Beneath the Surface

The Boat

I love to fish. I'm not that good and certainly don't catch some of the amazing fish you see in the sports magazines, but I have to admit, there are few things more relaxing than wading in an Arkansas river and fishing. No noise, no discussion, just nature and the rhythm of the cast.

I wasn't always this way. When I was a kid, I had the attention span of a gnat (not sure it is much better as an adult) and fishing required too much time and patience. I remember spending time in a flat-bottom boat with my dad as he fished, and as a kid, I spent most of my time playing with the rubber worms in the tackle box.

When I was about three years old, my dad was fishing in the Ouachita river in Arkansas, and as the boat drifted under a tree, I reached up, grabbed the branch, and was jerked out of the boat and into the water. With a lifejacket and dad's quick reflexes, I was quickly pulled back into the boat. That experience taught me one important lesson: *The boat is a place of safety.*

Unfortunately, everyone learns this lesson – and few unlearn it. It is a lesson that is not true.

Peter

A couple of thousand years ago, Peter, one of Jesus' disciples, had an interesting boat experience as well – his much more dramatic than mine. Peter didn't fall out of a boat – he stepped out, and that is how one of the most interesting stories in the New Testament unfolds:

Immediately after this, Jesus insisted that his disciples get back into the boat and cross to the other side of the lake, while he sent the people home. After sending them home, he went up into the hills by himself to pray. Night fell while he was there alone.

Meanwhile, the disciples were in trouble far away from land, for a strong wind had risen, and they were fighting heavy waves. About three o'clock in the morning Jesus came toward them, walking on the water. When the disciples saw him walking on the water, they were terrified. In their fear, they cried out, "It's a ghost!"

But Jesus spoke to them at once. "Don't be afraid," he said. "Take courage. I am here!"

Then Peter called to him, "Lord, if it's really you, tell me to come to you, walking on the water."

"Yes, come," Jesus said.

So Peter went over the side of the boat and walked on the water toward Jesus. But when he saw the strong wind and the waves, he was terrified and began to sink. "Save me, Lord!" he shouted. Jesus immediately reached out and grabbed him.

"You have so little faith," Jesus said. "Why did you doubt me?" (Matthew 14: 22-31).

With a first read, it is easy to think the main point of this story is to show Jesus' power over the natural world. After all, Jesus is Immanuel, "God with us," and so the idea that God himself can walk on the water and give another person that ability isn't hard to believe. At first glance, that seems to be the point of the story – Jesus allowed Peter to walk on the water and Peter should have had more faith. Simple enough.

But that is not all there is to this story. Rather, I'd say this story has one of the most complicated and compelling principles for our lives. The principle is this: To be close to Jesus, you have to get out of the boat.

Your Boats

Try to remember the first time you were scared. Think back as far as you can. Odds are, you can remember an event, a time, a place – perhaps even a nightmare—that scared you when you were a kid. Fear is a normal part of life and it doesn't take us long to experience fear. Some fear is, of course, necessary in life. Fear is what keeps you from driving your car off a cliff or touching your hand to a hot stove. Yet, fear becomes much more than a natural protective mechanism God has given us. Too often, fear becomes a motivator for the decisions we make in our lives. Rather than depending on Jesus, we all too often measure life's decisions based on "risk" and not by what God is calling us to do in our lives. This is how we end up in *spiritual boats* in the first place.

The Deep

Peter's experience involved a real wooden boat on a large lake at night in the middle of a storm. This real experience is a metaphor for all of our lives. In our lives, we probably won't find ourselves in a wooden boat on a lake in the middle of a stormy night with Jesus walking on the water, but all of us construct spiritual boats in our lives. But like Peter, we will have to abandon the boats in our lives if we want to be where Jesus is.

Jesus is never in the spiritual boats we create; he is always on the water of our lives.

So, what do these spiritual boats look like in our lives? A spiritual boat is a place of perceived safety. It is a place you put yourself in order to feel safe in the world around you. So, the boat you put yourself in has everything to do with what you fear, and there are, of course, many spiritual boats. A few common ones...

➤ Money & Possessions. Many Christians end up in the "boat" of money and possessions. The routine of life is mostly this: you work to make money so you can buy the things you want and need. Then you work to make more to take care of the things you have bought, replace the things that have worn out, and acquire more things along the way. You are "successful" if you acquire many things over the course of your life. You are especially successful if the people around you are impressed with the things you have. However, what happens is these "things" end up being a spiritual boat – in other words, they end up owning and controlling you. Of course, we all have to work and take care of the things of life, but a constant question we have to ask ourselves concerns our hearts. Are our hearts focused on the Kingdom of God or our kingdoms?

As Jesus said, you can't serve both God and money (see Matthew 6:24). You end up more dependent on money and possessions to protect and take care of your needs, rather than God. Not sure if you're in this boat? Ask yourself this question: If God led you to sell everything you own and use the money to move to a different city to help start a new church, would you? If you would, how hard would it be to step out of the boat?

➤ Pleasure & Comfort. It is a natural human desire to enjoy life and be comfortable. In fact, I would go so far as to say that the overwhelming majority of things that we buy have more to do with pleasure and comfort than necessity. Like money and possessions, there is nothing wrong with Godly pleasure and comfort in our lives. Yet, too often, the pursuit of personal pleasure becomes the driving force in our lives, rather than the pursuit of God's Kingdom. Far too often, people who claim to love Jesus and want to follow him turn away from him as soon as things get a bit uncomfortable. This happened when Jesus was here as well. A big group of people were following him and witnessing all the miracles and excitement. Then, the Scripture tells us, "*At this point, many of his disciples turned away and deserted him.*" (See John 6 to read the entire story.) The point is this: All of us have a tendency to stop following Jesus when things get uncomfortable. But here's the challenge: Find someone in the Bible who followed Jesus and also lived a life of complete pleasure and comfort. You won't find that person, and you won't be that person either if you get out of the boat.

➤ Relationships. As humans, we're relational beings, and that's no surprise because God is a relational God and we're made in his image. Jesus' work on the cross is, in the end, about God's work to save broken relationships with us. Without Jesus' blood, there would be no forgiveness of our sins and no healed relationship with God. Because of Christ, we can experience forgiveness and rebirth and reside in an eternal relationship with our creator. That eternal relationship should drive everything we do, but as sinners, we have a tendency to substitute our relationship with God for relationships with other people. It is good to have family, friends, to get married, and have children. But, our relationships with others should not trump our relationship with God. In fact, I would say that so many times, we end up in a relationship boat where everyone else in our lives is more important than God, and we can't have a deep relationship with God until the other relationships in our lives are in the right place (see Luke 9).

Of course, there are many other spiritual boats you might build for yourself. Anything that makes you feel safe, protected, and keeps you from really following God in your life is a spiritual boat. Here's what you should do: Stop reading right now and ask yourself what spiritual boats you have built. What do you depend on more than God? What keeps you from following God in your life? What fear motivates you to stay in your boats?

Those are hard questions, and you may not like the answers you get back. But you have to ask them and you have to be honest with yourself. Then, you must face this fact: *The spiritual boats you have created aren't real.*

Boat Myths

My wife and I have been fortunate enough to take our two kids on a couple of Caribbean cruises. Cruise ships are monstrous structures – floating cities really – and we had fun on each trip. At our family cabin in Arkansas, we have a canoe. So, what's the difference between a cruise ship and a canoe? Nothing really. When you break it all down, they are both simply boats, and a boat is a structure that is designed to keep you out of the water. The two boats are used in different ways for different purposes, but they both do the same thing.

You create spiritual boats in your life to keep you out of the water. In your mind, the "water" is a place of uncertainty, a place where you're really not that safe. Peter had to go through a mental struggle when he stepped out of a perfectly good boat and into the black water of night in the middle of a storm. After all, he ended up on the water because he asked Jesus if he could go there – not because he was forced.

Many times, you're going to be invited to step into the spiritual water of life – a place of uncertainty and perceived risk. Jesus is going to ask you to abandon the boats you have built for the water – a place where you'll have to depend on him in order to be close to him. A place where you can really grow in your relationship with him. A place where you can make a difference in eternity…

The problem is the boat. The boat is what keeps you from following Jesus and walking with him because you depend on the boat more than him.

To break out of this mentality, you have to realize two important issues with your boat:

Your boat keeps you contained.
Your boat can sink.

The Deep

The cruises we've been on were tons of fun. After all, the floating city had plenty of things to do – it was big with plenty of food and a good place to sleep. It had everything you needed to live and be entertained. Yet, something happened on each cruise. After four days, I started feeling antsy. By the fifth day, I was ready for the cruise to be over. I was climbing the walls. Even though the ship had everything I needed, I came to realize one simple reality: I was trapped.

And that is the reality of the boat: the boat keeps you out of the water but at the same time it traps you. When you're in a boat, you don't really go anywhere, and that is exactly where so many people are in their lives with Christ. You go to work, take care of your family, vacuum the carpet – you have everything you need in your life, but you feel like climbing the walls.

The odds are good that you feel like you are trapped because you are. You're in a spiritual boat. You secretly long for more, for some life that matters, for some adventure of a lifetime. Yet, God is calling you to a great mission with him – a mission that reaches to the heart of people – a mission that matters in eternity. It is the great mission for the human heart and we are called, commissioned, and commanded to go into the world and preach the gospel (see Matthew 28: 16-20). Regardless of your role in this great calling, you are called to reach into the world and help bring people to the cross. That calling is impossible to live out if you are sitting in a boat because that calling requires faith and motion. You can't serve Jesus and not trust him.

Many people are in a spiritual boat, but many churches are as well. Many churches are in "maintenance mode." They are simply trying to keep the church machine running effectively until everyone dies off. That sounds brutal, but it is a sad reality. Like us, churches can end up in spiritual boats when they become immobilized by fear. It takes big dreams and big risk to reach the lost and grow the church – you can't do it in a boat. When a church becomes more concerned about taking risks than following Jesus, it stops following Jesus and therefore it stops doing what Jesus calls us to do.

In your life, you'll end up doing the same thing. You'll start trusting in the things and people around you rather than God. When that happens, you're effectively trapped in your boat – immobilized – unable to follow Jesus who is not going to sit in your boat with you. And that is exactly where Satan wants you to be. Fear is a great motivator, and if Satan can keep you afraid of walking on the spiritual water in your life – afraid of risking it all for Jesus – he's got you exactly where he wants you. He will lie to you constantly about your boat and your need to stay in the boat because that's what he's good at – lying. Jesus said about Satan, *"When he lies, it is consistent with his character, for he is a liar and the father of lies."* (John 8:44).

So, when you're in the boat, Satan will lie to keep you there. Your own fear and desire will keep you there. And yet, you still hear Jesus calling to you from the water...

In the end, our spiritual boats aren't real. They're not real because none of them can protect us. Spiritual boats sink.

You depend on your money and possessions and trust in them to keep you safe, but you can lose every dollar and every possession in a matter of one day. Many people have. Even if you don't, you're not taking them with you – you came here naked and you'll return to the earth the same way. You can depend on pleasure and comfort, but those feelings can easily change – your situation can change. Your earthly relationships aren't permanent – any of them can change.

Your spiritual boats will sink.

The Water

My family loves cats and we have several. One thing about cats that has always fascinated me is how a cat will curiously stick its paw into a hole or a crack and paw around. I've always thought, "There is no way I would stick may hand in a hole and feel around in it without looking inside first." We're like that in life, aren't we? We want to know what is going to happen. We're not real good about sticking our hands into holes or stepping out of our boats onto the water. The funny thing: what we don't want to do is often exactly what Jesus will call us to do.

The "water" in this great metaphor is the great adventure of life. It is a place where the task Jesus calls you to is impossible without him. It is a place where, without him, you will sink. That was Peter's physical experience – it was not possible for him to walk on the water without Jesus. That is also a spiritual truth for us – we can't walk on the water in our own lives without Jesus lifting us up. It is more than we can do on our own, and for that reason, most of us spend our lives sitting in a boat. And yet...

In the boat, it is impossible to become what Jesus wants you to become...

In the boat, it is impossible to serve Jesus...

In the boat, it is impossible to really depend on God and see him work in your life...

In the boat, it is impossible to have a life that means something in the end...

The water is a place of great risk and danger. A place where you have to depend on Jesus in order to follow him. It is the place where life happens.

Fix Your Eyes

We come to Jesus in faith. After all, we don't see Jesus, but we believe in him and we believe what the Bible tells us – that salvation is in him and him alone. We must come as "little children" to him with a child-like faith, surrendering our hearts and lives to him – asking his forgiveness of our sins.

So, why then do we have such a problem depending on him for everything else? We depend on Jesus for our eternal destination, so why don't we depend on him today? And yet, the Bible is very clear...

➤ For by grace you have been saved through faith.... (Ephesians 2:8).
➤ Without faith, it is impossible to please God. (Hebrews 11:6).
➤ The just shall live by faith. (Habakkuk 2:4).

Peter's story is the story of a miracle and faith. He wanted to be where Jesus was, and Jesus was on the water. Jesus told him to come. He stepped out of his boat and started walking on the water. When he started noticing the wind and waves around him, he took his eyes off Jesus and started to sink. Yet, Jesus lifted him up and asked a simple but profound question that all of us have problems answering in our lives, "Why did you doubt?"

Jesus calls us to a radical life of following him. As believers, we want to be where Jesus is – we want to be close to him. But Jesus will always call us to walk a life of faith where we have to fix our eyes on him. Sure, we're human and we'll start to sink from time to time, but he will lift us up, correct us, love us, and we'll start again. That is the beauty of life out of the boat – it is a life where you get to be close to Jesus – a life where you can fix your eyes on him and nothing else. It's the life you've always wanted.

Steps

In this discussion, you have probably already identified a boat or two in your life. You probably see something that you fear, something you won't give up, something that has you trapped in your relationship with Jesus.

So, here's the challenge – take a step over the side of your boat. Put your foot in the water. Move your feet. Ask Jesus for a challenge, a risk, something he wants you to do. Something that without him, you will fail.

Give up something that is keeping you from loving your spouse in the same way Jesus loves you.

The next time your pastor says, "We need someone to…" be like Isaiah and say, "Here am I. Send me." Stretch – do something for God's Kingdom you've never done.

Sell something you own and give the money to a church planter or a missionary. Give the money to the children's ministry at your church. Better yet, give the money and then roll up your sleeves. Go help a missionary or a new church. Experience the thrill of being in the trenches – when someone steps over the line and is reborn. Experience the sorrow from God's heart when the people you have tried to reach won't believe.

Challenge yourself to really follow Jesus, take a risk, move your feet. As you do, fix your eyes on Jesus and abandon the boat.

And remember – when you walk on the water in your life, you get to walk right beside Jesus.

2

At The End of Your Rope

You've been there. If you haven't, you will. It is the space just between sanity and insanity. The space between hope and defeat. It is the space between the known and unknown. I'm talking about the end of your rope.

We reach the proverbial end of the rope when a situation in life takes us to a place of intense frustration or perceived failure. You may have been at the end of your rope with your job, a relationship, or a physical or emotional problem. The potential list of things that can take you to the end of your rope goes on and on.

Of course, the things that don't matter never take you to the end of your rope – the daily grind kind of stuff that may frustrate, but deep down you know it is not that important.

No, the stuff that takes you to the end of your rope is the important stuff, the stuff that does matter in your life, the stuff you love and care about.

The conventional wisdom: "When you reach the end of your rope, tie a knot and hang on."

The truth: "When you reach the end of your rope, let go."

Rahab

Here's a story about a prostitute, some guys, and a rope. Sounds like something you would see on a sleazy cable TV channel, but this story is straight out of your Bible and it is a story that has massive implications for us today:

Then Joshua secretly sent out two spies from the Israelite camp at Acacia Grove. He instructed them, "Scout out the land on the other side of the Jordan River, especially around Jericho." So the two men set out and came to the house of a prostitute named Rahab and stayed there that night.

But someone told the king of Jericho, "Some Israelites have come here tonight to spy out the land." So the king of Jericho sent orders to Rahab: "Bring out the men who have come into your house, for they have come here to spy out the whole land."

Rahab had hidden the two men, but she replied, "Yes, the men were here earlier, but I didn't know where they were from. They left the town at dusk, as the gates were about to close. I don't know where they went. If you hurry, you can probably catch up with them." (Actually, she had taken them up to the roof and hidden them beneath bundles of flax she had laid out.) So the king's men went looking for the spies along the road leading to the shallow crossings of the Jordan River. And as soon as the king's men had left, the gate of Jericho was shut.

Before the spies went to sleep that night, Rahab went up on the roof to talk with them. "I know the Lord has given you this land," she told them. "We are all afraid of you. Everyone in the land is living in terror. For we have heard how the Lord made a dry path for you through the Red Sea when you left Egypt. And we know what you did to Sihon and Og, the two Amorite kings east of the Jordan River, whose people you completely destroyed. No wonder our hearts have melted in fear! No one has the courage to fight after hearing such things. For the Lord your God is the supreme God of the heavens above and the earth below.

"Now swear to me by the Lord that you will be kind to me and my family since I have helped you. Give me some guarantee that when Jericho is conquered, you will let me live, along with my father and mother, my brothers and sisters, and all their families."

"We offer our own lives as a guarantee for your safety," the men agreed. "If you don't betray us, we will keep our promise and be kind to you when the Lord gives us the land."

Then, since Rahab's house was built into the town wall, she let them down by a rope through the window. "Escape to the hill country," she told them. "Hide there for three days from the men searching for you. Then, when they have returned, you can go on your way."

Before they left, the men told her, "We will be bound by the oath we have taken only if you follow these instructions. When we come into the land, you must leave this scarlet rope hanging from the window through which you let us down. And all your family members—your father, mother, brothers, and all your relatives—must be here inside the house. If they go out into the street and are killed, it will not be our fault. But if anyone lays a hand on people inside this house, we will accept the responsibility for their death. If you betray us, however, we are not bound by this oath in any way."

"I accept your terms," she replied. And she sent them on their way, leaving the scarlet rope hanging from the window. (Joshua 2:1-21).

Rahab had a choice. She could choose to stay in a dead life in a dead place - a life of prostitution in a city that was going to fall. We know from the Bible's record that Jericho did fall and it fell in a big way. She, along with the other people around her in the city, knew the reports she had heard. She knew about the Red Sea and how God delivered the Israelites in a miraculous way. She knew about other conquests God had given his people. She knew Jericho was next, just like everyone else around her. She let the spies out of the city with a scarlet rope, but in a very real sense, Rahab was the one who was at the end of her rope. She had a choice to make: choose death, or choose life.

The Challenge

In much the same way, we all start out life at the end of the proverbial rope. Though we look at a newborn baby with such hope and promise, the Bible's message to us is clear. We are all dead in our sins and trespasses (Ephesians 2:5) and we have no righteousness in and of ourselves (Romans 3:10). That's bad news because that means we are cut off and separated from God, who is holy in every way. Without God's intervention, our lives are hopeless, short, and without any meaning.

Our sin has to be reckoned with, and that is not a task we can pull off. Yet, because of God's great love for us, the Bible tells us that our sins can be erased, forgiven, and we can be reconciled to God forever because of the sacrifice Jesus made on the cross. When we turn from sin and turn to him, the Holy Spirit regenerates us, which effectively brings us back from the dead, and we enter into a new life in Christ (see Romans 6). This dead life we start with – the end of the rope – can be a new life and a new beginning in Christ if we turn to him.

Yet, once we are reborn, our lives don't turn into a rose garden where our purpose in life to is to drift along until we reach heaven. Rather, our lives should become powerful examples of the new life Christ as given us – we are called to be witnesses of this new life and God calls us to work with him as he seeks sinners to save and bring into his eternal Kingdom.

Yet, along this journey—this walk—this relationship with Christ—he will bring us to places where we must once again face the end of a rope. A place of change as he works to change us. And as believers, we are once again faced with the end of the rope in our lives.

Here's the deal, I've often found in my own life that God presents us with a series of "breaking points" over the course of our lives. Places where we are going to have to trust him in order to move forward in our lives. Sometimes we tend to stall out in these places until we learn to trust, but God will always bring us back to a place where we are forced to let go of the ropes and trust in him instead. I've experienced these personal breaking points through personal problems, dead-end jobs, and eventually a call to start a new church. In each of these situations, I've always had the choice to walk by faith, or walk by my own sight. I've had the choice to hang onto the end of the rope, or let go and trust Jesus. You will have the same opportunity in life as God works to refine you.

Go back to Rahab's story for a moment. If you think through the events that happened, there were only three basic questions she had to answer – and they are the same questions you will face time and time again in your life:

Will you trust God when no one else around you will?

Will you trust God's protection and deliverance, even when you're not sure if it's possible?

Will you trust in God's plan, even when you don't know what it is?

Want a close relationship with God – one that is deep? You'll answer these questions time and time again.

Trust

Trust is a funny thing. We start out life easily trusting those around us, such as our parents. Yet, something happens to us. We learn to… doubt. We learn that life is not as certain as we thought when we were kids and we learn that people can't always be depended on. We learn to doubt the world around us and we learn to doubt the people around us as well. In many cases, this doubt is certainly justified. After all, we don't live in a world where you can trust everyone. The problem, however, is this: That natural tendency to doubt spills over into our relationship with God. Doubt causes us to lose faith when the road ahead is uncertain. Doubt causes us to question God's motives in our lives. Doubt causes us to even question our relationship with him. This is why God, as he continually pursues a love relationship with us, will take us to the end of the rope in our lives. He will put us in places where we must choose to believe in him.

So, let's think about those mind-blowing questions for a few moments – questions you'd rather not have to answer when the going gets tough in your life.

Will you trust God when no one else around you will? If that hasn't happened to you yet, it will. There is going to come a time where you need to stand up, move your feet, or speak up. And you'll do it alone while everyone either ignores, criticizes, or cowers. It will always come down to this: you'll have to choose God's approval or people's approval. Tough, but true.

Will you trust God's protection and deliverance, even when you're not sure if it's possible? With God, all things are possible – but that doesn't mean all things are easy from our point of view. To let go of the rope in your life, you will have to believe in God and rest in him. Someone once said to me, "God will not give you more than you can handle." Oh, yes he will! In fact, he will almost every time. He will always put you in a place where you have to trust. 1 Corinthians 10:13 tells us God will not let you be tempted more than you can stand. But I'm not talking about temptations here – I'm talking about life challenges – those situations where you don't know what to do or how to move forward. In those, God always wants you to walk by faith and depend on him – not in yourself.

Will you trust in God's plan, even when you don't know what it is? I wish God would give me a diagram for my life, but he doesn't work that way. Here's a thought – what if God is much more interested in *you* than a *plan*? What if God is much more interested in his relationship with you rather than what you can accomplish? What if God would rather you just follow him and not worry about the rest? Here's what I think: If we'll just strive to follow him every day, then God's plan is naturally going to work itself out.

A New Beginning

Wonder what happened to Rahab? If the Bible never told us anything else, then her story would be incomplete in so many ways. In the end, did it even matter?

The good news is God has let us know in the New Testament. Her name appears in Matthew 1 as a woman in the lineage of Jesus. She also appears two more times in the New

Testament, named as an example of faith for us to follow (see Hebrews 11:31 and James 2:25).

Think about it – a prostitute in a doomed city who decided to let go of the personal rope in her life and open herself to an entirely new world – a *real* life.

And so, when you feel your fingers slipping off those last pieces of thread from the personal rope you're clinging to, remember this: You'll feel like you're falling, but actually, you're finally moving forward.

Let go and live.

Blue Rose

"Blue" is one of nature's more interesting colors because you see it in the sky and ocean, but not often in plants and flowers. Sure, there are a few, but not many plant species offer a "true blue" flower. My wife and I enjoy gardening and have a nice collection of rose bushes. You see all of the colors you might expect from a rose garden – but what about blue? Not so common, but there is a very pale lavender rose bush you can buy that is about as blue as a rose can get.

"That looks like something you would see at a funeral," my grandmother remarked when I showed her a photo of a blue rose in a gardening magazine. She was right. It had a certain somber look about it. No matter, I knew I would want one so I filled out the order form and one was on the way in no time.

The Deep

It turned out that the blue rose was exactly what was advertised. This rose really was blue. But I also found out something else. The rose wasn't particularly hardy. It seemed there was always something wrong, something withering, spotty or missing leaves, and the list went on and on. I kept it alive for several years but I spent more time taking care of it than I did all of the other roses combined. But when something is rare, beautiful, and unusual, you tend to spend the time nurturing, protecting, and caring for it.

Hebrews 11:6 tells us, *"And it is impossible to please God without faith. Anyone who wants to come to him must believe that God exists and that he rewards those who sincerely seek him."*

You've probably heard that scripture before. In fact, the Bible is full of scripture about faith and examples of people who had to live in faith. In other words, we have to do the same. And so, when you read this scripture, you know that you can't please God in your life without faith, so you think, "I just need to have faith."

Easy enough.

At least it *seems* easy enough. Let's face it – faith is very easy when everything is fine in your life. When things are not fine, faith is suddenly much more difficult. You lose your job, your marriage, your health, a loved one... and Jesus says "don't worry about tomorrow" and the Bible says, "don't lean on your own understanding."

Let's drop the "church-ese" for a moment and get real – faith is a roller coaster ride that never ends. One moment following God is pleasant and in another, you want to run screaming down the street. Life – the real roller coaster ride.

To add to the normal ups and downs, faith building and faith shattering experiences you'll go through, we have to also remember that Satan is constantly at work to try and undermine your faith. He'll do everything possible to force you to stop trusting in God, stop following, stop believing – to stall out. If he can do that, then he doesn't have to worry about you having that deep relationship after all.

Here's the mistake I think we all make. You have to have "saving faith" as it is called. You have to believe that Jesus died and rose again and that he is able to save you. Often, we have saving faith, but our faith waivers as we consider the fear of the day. In other words, subconsciously we believe that Christ saves us for all eternity – but we won't trust him with our cares and worries today. I've been there – you've been there – we'll both be there again at some point.

We need to stop thinking of faith as an *action* and instead as a *characteristic* of who we are – who Christ is refining us to be. But we have to realize the characteristic of faith is rare – it is unusual – and it is something Satan and the world will try to kill in your life. And so, faith has to be protected, it has to be nurtured, it has to be cared for. It is fragile and always under attack. Yet, that fragile faith God has put in our hearts is also the most beautiful thing ever.

That's what faith is like. It's like a blue rose.

Part 2

Exhale

The Extra Mile

A few years ago after quite a few years of neglect, I decided to get back in shape. Lots of hard work, dedication, and time are required in a weight loss endeavor. You have to keep pushing yourself to the next step.

I started out by walking a few miles most every day – and I found myself losing some weight and feeling better. But God designed our bodies to be very resilient. Soon, I wasn't losing any weight or making progress at all. The problem? I was still walking the same distance. To step it up, I would have to add more. So, I added another mile to what I was already walking – and it was tough. Just adding that extra mile that first time really wore me out. Of course in time, I adapted to the new mile and before long, it was easy. But then, I had to add another extra mile and the process started all over again.

There's a story in the New Testament that is inserted into a bigger story, so much so that I've read the passage numerous times and missed it numerous times. For some reason, one day God really hit me with this story. I found it amazing and I found it difficult—I found it beautiful.

This story is a part of Paul's conversion on the road to Damascus and involves a man named Ananias (not the Ananias and Sapphira story – that's a different guy).

Take a look at the story here:

Now there was a believer in Damascus named Ananias. The Lord spoke to him in a vision, calling, "Ananias!"

"Yes, Lord!" he replied.

The Lord said, "Go over to Straight Street, to the house of Judas. When you get there, ask for a man from Tarsus named Saul. He is praying to me right now. I have shown him a vision of a man named Ananias coming in and laying hands on him so he can see again."

"But Lord," exclaimed Ananias, "I've heard many people talk about the terrible things this man has done to the believers in Jerusalem! And he is authorized by the leading priests to arrest everyone who calls upon your name."

But the Lord said, "Go, for Saul is my chosen instrument to take my message to the Gentiles and to kings, as well as to the people of Israel. And I will show him how much he must suffer for my name's sake."

So Ananias went and found Saul. He laid his hands on him and said, "Brother Saul, the Lord Jesus, who appeared to you on the road, has sent me so that you might regain your sight and be filled with the Holy Spirit." Instantly something like scales fell from Saul's eyes, and he regained his sight. Then he got up and was baptized. Afterward he ate some food and regained his strength. (Acts 9: 10-19).

Think about it this way: You're going about your daily routine and God comes to you and says, "Hey, I want you to go help a terrorist."

That's basically what happened to Ananias.

Terrorism

Terrorism is something we're all familiar with in this post 9/11 age. By definition, terrorism means "the use of violence to intimidate or coerce." Today, when someone says "terrorism," we think of al-Qaeda. A couple of thousand years ago when someone said "terrorism," people thought of Paul.

Paul was a man on a mission. In the book of Acts, he tells us that he was a Pharisee, trained by the best religious teachers. He participated in the murder of Stephen and was determined to do his part to stamp out Christianity. He saw it as a threat to his religious beliefs, and his main tactic was violence and intimidation. In other words, he thought if you threatened Christians enough, the movement would eventually die out. In short, he was a terrorist against the early church.

Terrorists in your Life

Shift gears. You probably don't have a terrorist trying to stamp out Christianity in your life and threatening to kill you. Yet, if we think about it, there is another kind of terrorism in our lives. It's a terrorism that threatens to destroy our faith – our very walk – with God. Soft people in soft churches tend to call these things "distractions." I call them *terrorists* because they use "harm" to try and separate you from God:

> ➤ Complacency: Complacency is a feeling of "self-sat-isfaction." In a nutshell, it means that you're happy with the way things are. As such, you won't put any effort into making changes to your life. In America, it is very easy for Christians to be complacent. We go to church, pay the tithe (maybe), get involved or not, drift along… and that's about it. If that sounds harsh, it is just a reality. I know too many complacent Christians and too many complacent churches whose main goal is to keep things the way they are and not rock the boat. But… sometimes the boat needs to be rocked. Sometimes being "happy" and comfortable isn't the best place to be. Sometimes safety is really just another word for fear. In other words, think of it this way: how can God "conform you to the image of Christ," as the Bible says, if you won't allow him to change you? You can't. You can't follow God with-out risk. You can't follow God without change. You can't follow God if you're happy with the status quo. Complacency is a terrorist.

> ➤ Fear: As humans, we need certain kinds of fear in our lives. Fear keeps you from sticking your face in a fire-place or jumping off a building "just to see what will happen." Without that kind of fear, you won't live long. But a secondary kind of fear is really a fear of the unknown. We all have it – we all like to pretend we don't – but nevertheless, fear is something we have to contend with. Sadly, fear is also what keeps many people from following God and walking with

him. Fear about your future is really a lack of trust in God. If you are so afraid that you won't follow God's leading, then Satan will use that fear to keep you immobile – sort of like the way a spider wraps an insect in a web. In other words, Satan uses fear to keep you afraid so that you don't actually do anything God wants you to do in your life. Think about it this way: Fear is really a kind of faith. It's just faith in the wrong thing.

➤ Lust: The Bible speaks in many passages about lust and sexual sin. Many people read those passages and think of God as a cosmic killjoy who doesn't want people to enjoy life and have fun. The Bible's goal is to help you understand what is sexual sin for one simple reason: Sexual sin is devastating to your life and your heart. The Bible's primary advice: Act like Joseph and run (see Genesis 39 and 1 Corinthians 6:18). The problem with lust and sexual sin is the fallout – it's devastating. It destroys families and ministries. It's subversive. For so many Christians who have gotten caught in the lust web, they know all too well the terrorism of lust and sexual sin.

➤ The Television: You may think it's odd that I mention TV here. I have a TV, you have one (or more) as well. We all watch it. The problem is TV can be good, but all too often, the shows we watch push a world view that is anti-God and certainly anti-Biblical. So many prime time TV shows and even commercials are shockingly sexual in nature and most present life ideals that are very far from God. I'll not harp on the subject, but in the end, here it is: If you want to drift far from God, just spend most of your time with a TV. You see, you tend to adopt into your mind and heart what you see and hear. (1 Corinthians 6: 9-12).

➤ Friends & Family: Oddly, friends and family can be a terrorist in your life. Think of it this way, your friends and even family members – the people closest to you – can sabotage your relationship with God and pull you away from him. The question you have to stop and ask yourself from time to time is this: Who am I close to that is pulling me away from God? A tough question. An important question.

Back to Ananias

So, God essentially told Ananias to help a terrorist. Ananias even reminds God of all the terrible things Paul had done (as if God needed a reminder). In other words, Ananias receives the call from God, offers an objection, and God again tells Ananias what to do—which was no different than what God first said (I imagine God wanting to say here, "Did I stutter?").

We read in our Bibles the rest of the story. Ananias went to Paul, Paul got his eyesight back, Paul was baptized, and Paul later becomes this massive force in the world for the church. Ananias' story is easy for us *because we already know the outcome of the story.* In your life, it's not that simple, now is it? It wasn't that simple for Ananias either because he didn't know how the story was going to work out.

He didn't know God had already been making a way to reach out to Paul.

He didn't know what Paul might do.

All he knew is God told him to go help a terrorist.

The Extra Mile

I love the beach – so do my wife and kids. Hawaii is one of our favorite places in the world and we try to go as often as possible. The only downside is the travel. From Texas, where I live, to Hawaii, you're looking at a nine hour plane ride, non-stop. During that flight, you jump through two time zones. On the way over, it's no big deal because you gain time. If the plane leaves at 10:00 a.m., you'll end up in Honolulu around 2:30 in the afternoon – even though you've been on the plane nearly nine hours. In other words, you get a really long day.

It's the ride home that gets interesting because you lose time. The plane typically lands at DFW airport at 5:00 am, but it's still the previous day to you – you haven't even gone to bed yet and it's already the next day when you get home. It's a weird feeling – it's the only time I feel like I can travel through time. I'm still in "yesterday," but I already know what is going to happen "tomorrow" because I'm there too. It will mess with your mind a bit.

In life, you are where you are. It's your today. You know about yesterday, and you know about today, at least up until the very moment. Your tomorrow is a shady character – you have no idea what's going to happen.

The thing is, God is the only real time traveler. He's in your yesterday, your today, but he's already in your tomorrow. In other words, the future is the same to God as the past – no difference to him. In fact, when God talked about things that *would* happen in the Bible, he often spoke of them as if they had *already* happened. In our world, everything is measured by space and time, but God is not limited to that. So the simple principle is this: In your life, no matter what's going on, God already knows what is going to happen in your tomorrow.

The Deep

So, in Ananias' case, God already knew that Ananias was in no danger and he already knew that Paul was a "chosen vessel," so why didn't he just explain that to Ananias and remove all of the stress?

Because. *If he had, then the knowledge would have removed the power of the Extra mile.*

When I preach, I often use the concept of "God e-mail." In other words, I say things like, "I wish God would send me an e-mail and just tell me what I should do." It makes a good analogy about how we want to know what steps to take in difficult situations.

The truth, though, is we really don't need an email from God. What we need is the wisdom to do what he has already told us to do from his word and the ability to be still before him so the Spirit can lead us.

God's greater desire in our lives isn't that we follow a set of instructions, or get an easy pass, or never struggle – His desire is that we walk with him. If he spells out the future for us, then we need no faith. We need no dependency. We need no trust.

"Why doesn't God just tell me what to do? Why doesn't God just let me know what is going to happen?"

He doesn't because of us. He doesn't for the sake of our relationship with him. Instead, he sometimes requires us to walk an extra mile of faith in our lives to help us grow and depend on him more.

Like an exercise program, that extra mile is a stretch. It's tough. It pushes the boundaries of faith. It's tiring – and often, unknown.

At the end of the day, Ananias had a decision to make. He had to decide if he would walk an extra mile of faith with God. I wonder what all went through his mind as he walked toward Straight Street, to Judas' house where Paul was waiting.

I wonder what fear, I wonder what questions, I wonder how he tried to make sense of it all.

But the important thing isn't that he may have feared or that he may have had questions. The important thing is that he kept walking. He kept believing. He kept hoping. He kept his faith.

Ananias had to make a decision to move his feet.

Sometimes, you'll have to do the same.

Bread

Think about a loaf of bread. You eat it, you throw the scraps out, you may skip over the heels. If the bread gets a little old, you simply discard it. In a land with a lot of food, you probably don't spend much time thinking about bread.

But let's change the scenario. Let's say there is a great famine. Now, you're down to one piece of bread in your household. It's not enough to feed everyone. Your sister is very weak and needs the bread, but she is likely to die anyway – even with the bread. Do you give her the bread or do you save the bread for yourself and others who are still healthy? Whose life do you save? In the famine, the bread means everything, but it is full of difficult moral questions.

Jesus understood the concept of needing bread. He also understood that Satan will try to build a web of deceit in a time of great need. Here's what happened:

Then Jesus was led by the Spirit into the wilderness to be tempted there by the devil. For forty days and forty nights he fasted and became very hungry.

During that time the devil came and said to him, "If you are the Son of God, tell these stones to become loaves of bread."

But Jesus told him, "No! The Scriptures say,

'People do not live by bread alone, but by every word that comes from the mouth of God.' " (Matthew 4: 1-4).

Notice how Jesus had been in the wilderness for 40 days and nights, notice how he had been fasting. Notice how just at the right time Satan showed up with a temptation – a deception – based on exactly what Jesus needed at the moment. There's a reason this story is in the Bible. You'll find this same Satan web trying to step into your life time and time again.

Deception

It's important to understand how Satan works. Satan is a not a red character with horns and a pitch fork who is hiding behind a trash can in the grocery store parking lot, waiting to jump out and say, "Boo!" Silly, but all too often, we downplay the work of Satan in our lives. We reduce him to some stereotypical spiritual character instead of taking him seriously. Jesus took him seriously and had some important things to tell us about Satan. Jesus described him this way:

He was a murderer from the beginning. He has always hated the truth, because there is no truth in him. When he lies, it is consistent with his character; for he is a liar and the father of lies. (John 8:44).

What Jesus wants you to know is simply this: Satan will try to invade your life with lies and deception. He will tempt you with lies, he will help you believe things that are false with lies, he will make you angry with lies – the list goes on and on.

So, think about this: What makes a good lie? A good lie always:

A. Sounds plausible.
B. Feels right.
C. Uses some truth mixed with untruth.

That's the approach Satan tried to take with Jesus – it's the same approach he'll use in your life as well.

Jesus Responds

Jesus responds with a very telling answer when Satan tempts him. Jesus responds not with his own rebuttal, but he simply responds by quoting the Bible. When Jesus says, "People do not live by bread alone…" he is quoting Deuteronomy 8:3. His response to Satan is to quote the Bible to him for the answer – and for one simple reason. The Bible is the truth of God, and Satan's lies simply can't stand up to the truth. When you take his darkness and drag it into the light of God's word – the darkness vanishes. The Bible is truly more powerful than a two-edged sword. (Hebrews 4:12).

Now, here comes the preaching. Skip this if you want because if you read it, you're now accountable for it. Here it is: *We have no excuse for not knowing God's word.* Period. We live in the most Bible saturated society there ever has been. Consider these simple facts:

- You can buy a Bible. No one is going to arrest or kill you for having one (unlike some countries in the world).
- You can have more than one Bible if you want.
- You can get various Bible versions.
- You can get a Bible based on your reading ability.
- You can get a Bible in large print if you have trouble seeing.
- You can get a Bible in Braille if you are blind.
- If you don't have any money, any church will give you a Bible.
- You can read the Bible on the Internet for free, and in any version and in any language.
- You can get the Bible as an app for your phone / mobile device / iPod.
- Your phone / mobile device / iPod will read the Bible to you.
- You can get the Bible on CD and listen to it.
- Churches offer Bible studies and classes to help you understand the Bible.
- You can take Bible classes online.

…. should I keep going?

We have more technology today with more ways to put the word of God in your heart than ever before. Yet, we are the most Biblically illiterate generation that has existed in American history.

We are going to answer to God for that. We are accountable for not knowing his word considering how easily we can – if we want to.

Here's the last thing and then the preaching stops: *You can't resist the temptation of Satan and his lies in your life if you don't know what your Bible says.* No way, no how. Jesus quoted the scripture to Satan when Satan tried to get into his life—you had better be prepared to do the same.

Real Need... Fake Solution

Jesus was hungry – the need was real. After all, he had been fasting for 40 days with very little food. So, Satan simply reminds him that he has the power to turn some rocks into bread. Satan gives him an immediate solution to the problem... or so it seems.

Go back to the scripture for a moment. Matthew 4 begins by saying Jesus was led by the Spirit into the wilderness to be tempted, or tested. If Jesus jumps in with a solution to his hunger problem, he is basically violating the will of God, which was to endure this time of testing. See the dilemma? Satan's deceptive approach isn't to attack, but to lie. To spin doctor things. He simply reminds Jesus that he has a real need and he has the power to fix the need.

But the solution is a fake one – the solution Satan offers is a quick, empty solution. Sure, Jesus can create some bread, eat it, and be relieved of his hunger, but at what cost?

Satan will try to do the same thing in your life.

Hunger Pains

We're probably not too worried about being hungry – we live in a country with plenty of food. But "hunger" can be more than a need for food - hunger can be a need to satisfy any drive in your life where needs are not being met. *Bread* can also be more than food – it can be something that can meet a need in your life. Maybe the hunger in your life is intimacy, sex, friendships, to fit in, and the list can go on and on. Know this – the hunger can be real, there can be real bread for the hunger - but when you're hungry in your life, Satan will always step in with a temptation – a quick fix – for the hunger. The problem is this: Satan will appear to offer you bread (a solution), but what he really offers is a cookie (a quick fix).

Let me explain. Let's say you haven't eaten all day and it is now 3 p.m. You're going to feel pretty rotten. Your body, after all, is a fuel burning machine that has to be fed every so often. Once the fuel is depleted, you feel hungry and weak. You need food to replenish the fuel tank – good food. You need a balance of protein, carbs, healthy fats, vitamins, and the many other nutrients our bodies burn. But… what happens at the moment of great hunger if instead of eating a good meal, you eat a cookie? A cookie is mostly sugar and simple carbs.

But… it looks good, it tastes good – sweet and delicious.

You eat it. You get a surge of sugar in your blood-stream – a burst of energy. You think, "I feel great!"

The problem is your body will burn through the sugar and carbs in only a few minutes, and you feel a crash in your energy. In fact, you may feel worse than you did before you ate.

All of this happens because the cookie looks good, smells good, tastes good – *is tempting* – but it isn't real food. It can't fuel your body.

And that is what Satan does. In times of real need, Satan will always step in and offer you something that appears to be "bread," but in the end it is destruction. Satan always offers something deceptive.

Temptations

So, let's take that idea and apply it to a real world situation – a situation that happens often. Let's say that you're "hungry" in your marriage. Perhaps there are problems. Something has happened. Nevertheless, the marriage is lacking in intimacy and sex. The need for intimacy and sex is a real need that we have - it is something God designed into us. However, because that need is very strong, Satan can easily offer you things that appear to be bread. Things that appear to satisfy the need for intimacy and sex.

Satan will offer you an affair.

Satan will offer you porn.

These things appear to satisfy a real need – but they are simply cookies. They'll be exciting, seem good, but the effect doesn't last long. Then, because of the sexual sin, you'll have a laundry list of problems that will come out of them. That's how Satan works. He will always substitute real bread with a cookie. In this situation, what you really need is to take every possible step to restore the love relationship in the marriage rather than looking elsewhere to fill a need that can *only be* filled inside of the marriage.

See how it works? Satan is great at taking real "bread" needs and offering "cookies." You have to identify this maneuver in your life and realize that only real bread will satisfy.

" I Am the Bread "

Jesus said, "I am the bread of life." Of course, he isn't bread for the stomach, but he is bread for the soul. Real food – something that sustains for eternity. The longing you feel, the hunger you have, can only be fed by God through Jesus. There's no other way to fill that need.

So, the contrast is this: In your life, you're going to need an everlasting spiritual bread (Christ) and you're going to need physical bread for your stomach – and you'll need "bread" for other needs in your life, too.

Jesus offers all that you need. Satan offers a quick fix that won't last. You have to choose which one you'll take.

The question remains: What do you do when you're hungry in life? What if your marriage lacks intimacy? What if you need something more from life? What if there is a real hunger that just isn't getting met?

Here's the thing: When Jesus was in the desert, Satan offered him bread. Jesus refused the temptation. But he was still hungry. His hunger problem wasn't resolved—at least not right away.

Sometimes in life, God will allow you to walk through times of difficulty – times of trial – to build your faith. It's like building a muscle. If you want to build up your arms, you're going to have to lift some weights. You'll need to do that until they're exhausted. But, that's the only way muscles grow. They have to be challenged.

Sometimes, you need to be challenged. God will not always prevent Satan from offering you cookies. He'll let you see the offer, he'll make you face the temptation, but he promises to be with us during those times of trial. We just have to make the right decisions.

The good news is the desert doesn't last forever. Keep believing. Keep trusting. Keep walking in faith. Keep doing what is right. Keep praying. Continue knowing that the God of your today is the God of your tomorrow.

And remember this: *"Blessed is he who is hungry, for he shall be filled."* (Matthew 5:6).

No Escalator

DFW Airport is one of the larger airports in America. It's a "hub" airport, meaning that if you get on a flight from another airport in the general area, you may end up at DFW to catch a connecting flight. Because of this, DFW Airport is huge. In fact, it's bigger than Manhattan Island.

Like most airports, DFW contains multiple levels, from the ground floor up. On one trip, I came in at the ground floor, went up one floor and through security, realized they had changed the flight to a different gate, went up to another floor, then caught a tram, then went down a floor before finally arriving at the right place. Exhausting.

But... the trek around the airport could have been much worse. Thankfully, DFW is full of escalators so when you maneuver between floors, you don't have to actually climb any stairs. Imagine climbing those huge flights of stairs, up and down, with luggage.

Of course, life is not an airport.

There are no escalators in life.

You're going to travel a lot.

And you're going to drag luggage with you.

Luggage

We all have personal luggage. It's a part of being a sinner, living in a fallen world. When we put our faith and trust in Christ to save us, the Bible teaches that we are "made new," given a new heart for eternity – made clean. We are made clean by the righteous work of Jesus on the cross and by his resurrection – not because of anything we might do or have done. Thing is, when you are reborn, you don't get a new physical life, or a new environment to live in (at least not yet). You have to keep living here, in a world of sin and pain. You keep the same body (just check out the new wrinkles you probably acquired this past year – a sure sign of an aging body).

You also keep all of your memories, problems, personal temptations, and frailties. You carry a suitcase of stuff with you, and we have a very difficult time unloading the suitcases of our pasts, even though we have found new life in Christ. You have a great tendency to continue to carry with you:

- Guilt over your former life
- Guilt about past sin
- Hurt other people have inflicted on you
- Pride

- Fear
- Jealousy

You get the picture. We all have a suitcase – and unfortunately, we drag that suitcase – that luggage with us through life. And the load can get heavy. Especially when you're climbing stairs.

The Trash Factor

Our suitcases are our own doing. God doesn't want us dragging around the past with us and the Bible very succinctly points out an interesting principle:

Everything else is worthless when compared with the infinite value of knowing Christ Jesus my Lord. For his sake I have discarded everything else, <u>*counting it all as garbage,*</u> *so that I could gain Christ and become one with him… I focus on this one thing: Forgetting the past and looking forward to what lies ahead.* (Philippians 3: 8-13 paraphrased).

I like that – count it all as garbage, forget the past, look forward to what lies ahead. That sounds like a plan to me. But it's not that easy to do.

But what if we opened the suitcases of the past? What if you were brave enough to sit down with a piece of paper and a pencil in a quiet room? What if you were brave enough to write down the issues from your past that really plague you? What if you were brave enough to put those dark corners of your heart in written words where you could look at them? What if you were brave enough to open that suitcase?

You would find one thing: it's all garbage. All of the junk from the past that you keep dragging around with you is garbage – that's all it is.

You might say, "I was abused as a child – that's not garbage!" No, but the hurt and pain of it is—the Bible tells you that you are more than a conqueror through Jesus Christ (Romans 8:37). You see, the events of life that shape your feelings, your cares, and your worries are real, but the feelings from that past that are dragging you down today are garbage that needs to be thrown out. As the scripture tells us, we need to count the past as garbage and look to what is ahead. Far too often, it's the garbage of the past that keeps us from a deep relationship with God. In other words, think of it this way: Imagine God is on one side of the room and you are on the other. Too often, the space between is filled with garbage in your life, and it is that garbage that will often keep you from following him and living the dynamic life of faith he wants you to live.

The good news is the garbage we all carry tends to fall into a few categories. As you think about your life, you'll probably find that your suitcase garbage is primarily made of one of these four issues.

1. Anger (Be angry but do not sin... Eph 4:26)

Things happen. Life isn't fair. People aren't fair. You learn that from an early age. But sometimes people do things to you that you just have a hard time letting go of. So you hold onto the anger, then you box it down, then you suitcase it in your life – and you think you're over it when you have simply stored it away.

The problem is, anger will burn you up. I have a leather jacket I like to wear when I'm cold. Basically, a jacket is an article of clothing designed to help your body regulate temperature. When you're chilly, you put it on so you can warm up. When you get warm, you take it off to cool down.

Anger is a lot like that. Anger, in and of itself, is not wrong. Ephesians 4 tells us to "be angry but do not sin." In other words, if you're angry, let the anger drive you to right decisions, not sin, so that good changes can be made. For example, anger in a marriage is necessary. I get angry at my wife and she gets angry at me. But in our love relationship, that anger can be used in a positive way – to open the lines of communication. For better understanding. For changes in both of us. In the end, anger can help you make things better.

But too often, we hold onto anger rather than coping with it in a positive way and letting it go. The end result is the jacket effect – if you keep it on too long, you burn up. Maybe this is you. Maybe you have held onto long-term anger at a family member, a spouse, a child, a boss – the list is endless. There was a time when the anger could have helped – it could have driven you to make the right decisions. But once you suitcase the anger, the time for action has passed.

Now is the time for letting go. To be blunt, what do you want more? To stay angry at the person or to walk in freedom with God?

"But I don't know how…" Likely, some forgiveness has to take place. Read on…

2. Forgiveness (If you forgive those who sin against you, your heavenly father will forgive you. Matt 6:14)

Why is it that the forgiven have such a hard time forgiving?

Let's get real – you hate that statement, don't you? We usually do. We don't like being confronted with unforgiveness in our lives because the behavior of unforgiveness has such an impact on our walk with God. But you've had unforgiveness in your life – so have I. It has to be dealt with and there are no shortcuts.

At the heart of the matter, unforgiveness is really about "control." I know that seems hard to believe, but bear with me for a moment. Let's say someone does something to you. That person was wrong and your feelings of hurt and betrayal are justified. Let's also say that the person has never made things right – he or she has never asked to be forgiven. In this sort of situation, it is easy to hang onto unforgiveness – to package it up and keep it. After all, if you forgive the person who has hurt you, you let that person *win*. Unforgiveness feels like you keep the upper hand.

But hang on. We didn't "deserve" forgiveness and Christ forgave us. That's the first thing you must internalize. For the Bible tells us that even when we were still sinners, Jesus died for us. In other words, Jesus loved you before you ever loved him (see Romans 5:8 and 1 John 4:19). We need to do the same. Hard at times – yes. Required, yes.

But another "unforgiveness issue" is justice. When we are wronged, we want justice for the wrongdoing. I think this issue is why we often struggle with forgiving others in cases where the person hasn't made things right. If we forgive, then we give up control. If we forgive, then we feel like we let the person off the hook, free and clear.

When we feel this way, though, we're forgetting one fundamental principle. For the Lord says, "Vengeance is mine; I will repay" (see Romans 12: 19-21). In other words, "pay back" is not our responsibility or our right. Vengeance belongs to God.

So, the hard work of forgiveness is to realize it is not your place to hold the justice. Our response is to forgive, which effectively releases that person from your responsibility to God's care and justice. When you do that, you empty the unforgiveness from your life and walk in freedom. When you don't, you end up carrying something that doesn't belong to you – and it is something too heavy for you to carry. Unforgiveness burns you alive from the inside out.

3. Fear (God has not given you a spirit of fear... 2 Timothy 1:7)

If you've been reading this book in order, you know the subject of fear has already come up a few times. Fear is a major motivator in our lives. At times it is necessary, but in our spiritual lives, far too often, fear keeps us from following God. The scripture tells us that God has not given us a spirit of fear, but of power, love, and a sound mind. In other words, spiritual fear doesn't come from God. The fears we deal with in our lives come from our past, or just from our basic nature. We're afraid God will not protect us in our lives.

The hard work: We have to identify the things we fear, spiritually speaking, and strive to eject that fear from our lives. We have to depend on God's nature of grace, mercy and love toward us and understand that even in the dark times of our lives, God is for us, not against us.

After all, as the Bible tells us, perfect love casts out fear (1 John 4:18).

4. Pride (Humble yourselves before the Lord... James 4:10)

Pride, in a negative sense, is an elevated sense of one's self. Often, people are prideful because of their possessions or certain skills. If you have a nice car, you can be prideful of the possession. If you're a great basketball player, you can be prideful about the ability. We're all familiar with this kind of pride.

But there is a secondary kind of pride that goes deeper. It is a pride over our own weaknesses. As people, we don't like others to know about our struggles, and so we tend to mask those weaknesses to other people. Physical, emotional – this behavior runs the whole gamut. The problem is that we behave in the same way with God. We act like we have things under control in our lives so much that we have this same kind of behavior with God – who already knows the truth anyway.

We need to be more like Paul if we want to have dynamic faith. Instead of always trying to make ourselves at least appear stronger, we should admit and embrace the weakness.

Paul put it this way, *"That's why I take pleasure in my weaknesses, and in the insults, hardships, persecutions, and troubles that I suffer for Christ. For when I am weak, then I am strong."* (2 Corinthians 12:10).

See, Paul learned something very important. He learned that real strength isn't about being strong – it is about being dependent on Christ. When we can drop the fake face, accept our weaknesses and frailties, let go of our pride, then we can walk in freedom with Christ. Walking forward in our weaknesses requires faith. And faith, is how we walk with God in the first place.

Step Aerobics

So, back in the airport of life, there are no escalators. You have to climb up and down stairs, dragging your luggage along for the ride. Hopefully, you'll identify some of the junk luggage you have and take some steps of faith to lighten your load. But the fact remains: Walking in this life is a difficult journey.

Why?

God could have made life easier than it is. He could have removed the stairs of our lives and replaced them with escalators. We've been made new by the power of Christ's blood; our relationship with him is secure now and in eternity. So… why all of the struggle?

Think about it this way: Have you ever practiced calf exercises? Stand squarely on the floor and then raise yourself up on your tip-toes. Hold that position for a few seconds, then lower yourself. Now, do that forty times. What's going to happen? The next day, your calves will be sore. But, if you continue these calf exercises on a regular regime, they will stop being sore because they will adapt to the exercise. In fact, they will grow and become stronger.

Escalators don't work your heart. Stairs make you work. If you climb stairs regularly, you'll get stronger. This is true in our spiritual lives. God doesn't put us on an easy track because we won't grow in our faith and love him if everything is easy. We need the steps of faith. We need step aerobics of faith in order to grow.

The Bible calls this a refinement process. Take a look at this from 1 Peter 1: 6-9:

So be truly glad. There is wonderful joy ahead, even though you have to endure many trials for a little while. These trials will show that your faith is genuine. It is being tested as fire tests and purifies gold—though your faith is far more precious than mere gold. So when your faith remains strong through many trials, it will bring you much praise and glory and honor on the day when Jesus Christ is revealed to the whole world.

You love him even though you have never seen him. Though you do not see him now, you trust him; and you rejoice with a glorious, inexpressible joy. The reward for trusting him will be the salvation of your souls.

The reality is this: Spiritual step aerobics are often hard and scary, but we need them to be strong in the faith. We need them to be refined; we need them to grow.

The Hub

But there is one more important issue to consider. A question you may not like, but one we all need to stop and examine from time to time.

Returning to our airport scene: When you're in an airport, the purpose of the many stairs, elevators, and escalators is to take you to a gate so you can get on a plane. So you can fly. After all, no one goes to an airport for fun. In fact, no one really wants to be there at all. The purpose of the airport is to get you on a plane.

Many times, though, you'll end up at an airport like DFW because it is a hub. Let's say you want to fly from Oklahoma City to Honolulu. Problem is, you can't. You'll fly from

Oklahoma City to DFW, then onto Honolulu. Whether you want to or not, you'll end up going through the hub in order to fly where you want.

In our spiritual lives, you may find yourself at a hub from time to time. You may look across the distance in your life and see the person you long to be: a person of greater faith, of greater mission, of greater purpose. You want to fly from where you are to that other place – that greater place. But so often, you can't.

Instead, God will route you through a spiritual hub. It's a place where you have to find your way. A place with a lot of stairs. A place that's exhausting, trying, and frustrating. But you have to go through the hub in order to fly.

Sadly, this is a part of the journey where so many Christians get stuck in a limbo of life. God wants to refine them, to conform them to the image of his Son. But work is required. Step aerobics are necessary. So God takes you to a hub in your life. Too often though, many believers won't put down the luggage. They won't do the hard work of climbing stairs. They know where they want to go, but they find the journey too hard. So, they often settle for just living in the hub: a place where you just sort of fumble along through life. You pay the bills, go to work, raise the kids, mow the yard – but you always feel like something is missing. Like there is a greater mission – a greater space for you.

Could it be that you're trapped in a hub? Could it be that God has shown you some hard refinement work that needs to happen in your life, but you keep standing at the bottom of the stairs, hoping an escalator of faith will appear?

It's a hard question. It's one we have to be brave enough to answer – to look into the recesses of our lives and hearts and ask a profound question of God, "What do I need to do to grow?" You have to be brave to ask that question – you have to be willing to do the work.

But in the end, the only way to leave the hub is to climb the stairs. To find your way. To believe. To have faith. To be changed and refined.

Only then, can you fly.

Part 3

Descending

7

Waiting in the Garden

Just before Jesus was arrested, tried, and crucified, the Bible records a time of prayer in the Garden of Gethsemane. The garden was a place just outside of the city near the Mount of Olives. To the best of our speculation, it was a big area full of olive trees – a good place to be alone in the middle of the night.

Of course, Jesus prayed there. He was arrested there. The Bible tells us about a disciple cutting off the ear of one of the arresting centurions. You know the story. But, zero-in on this story for just a moment. The implications of it are astounding for our walk of faith:

Then Jesus went with them to the olive grove called Gethsemane, and he said, "Sit here while I go over there to pray." He took Peter and

The Deep

Zebedee's two sons, James and John, and he became anguished and distressed. He told them, "My soul is crushed with grief to the point of death. Stay here and keep watch with me."

He went on a little farther and bowed with his face to the ground, praying, "My Father! If it is possible, let this cup of suffering be taken away from me. Yet I want your will to be done, not mine."

Then he returned to the disciples and found them asleep. He said to Peter, "Couldn't you watch with me even one hour? Keep watch and pray, so that you will not give in to temptation. For the spirit is willing, but the body is weak!"

Then Jesus left them a second time and prayed, "My Father! If this cup cannot be taken away unless I drink it, your will be done." When he returned to them again, he found them sleeping, for they couldn't keep their eyes open.

So he went to pray a third time, saying the same things again. Then he came to the disciples and said, "Go ahead and sleep. Have your rest. But look—the time has come. The Son of Man is betrayed into the hands of sinners. Up, let's be going. Look, my betrayer is here!" (Matthew 26: 36-46).

We could talk about many issues just from this passage: pain, suffering, fear, prayer – many things. Instead, though, think about this issue: waiting… and sleeping. Far too often, we are like Jesus' disciples. We tire of waiting, and instead opt for "sleeping."

It's one of those things that truly keeps so many of us from living deep lives with God.

But I don't want to sleep.

I want to wait.

I want to be someone who would stay awake in the garden.

Auto Pilot

Today's commercial airliners are equipped with an auto pilot. For the most part, they basically fly themselves while in the air. Sure, the pilot has to be there, but so much of the flying is handled by the machine. I wish my car had one of those. I really don't like driving because you have to pay attention to what you're doing, and on a long trip, it is exhausting.

In our spiritual lives, we have a tendency to be on auto pilot. We do the things of life, take care of business, raise the kids, but we sort of sleep-walk through life. We read about the people in the Bible who had these dynamic relationships with Christ – it all seems so exciting. Then, we look at our 9 to 5 lives and wonder why things are so boring. Where is the God of the Bible in our lives?

God is exactly where he has always been – on the throne. Maybe it's not that God isn't doing anything. Maybe it's the auto pilot. Maybe it's the sleep walking.

Maybe we don't have the dynamic relationship we want with God because we're too concerned with how "easy" things are.

Easy Chair

Here's what I want: I don't want to have any major problems that I can't handle. I don't want to ever get sick. I want to have plenty of money. I don't want to have any problems with my wife and kids. I want my job to be fulfilling and easy… I want an easy chair.

Sound familiar? Be honest – those are the things we all want. I want to be on top of the mountain with the sunshine of God's love, grace, and mercy over me.

Of course, his love, grace, and mercy are always over me. But life is a not a sunny mountaintop – not all of the time. Sometimes you have to walk through the valley. Sometimes you have to be changed in the dark times of life. The easy chair mentality is just a myth because sometimes you have to wait on God instead.

The Waiting Game

But why wait?

God is God and he can do anything. If you have a need in your life and you ask God for help, his answer is sometimes "Yes" or "No," but so many times, the response is "Wait."

Why? I mean, if you're a parent, you give your kids what they need as soon as they need it, right? Or do you?

My youngest daughter had some money. But she didn't have enough – about half in fact – for what she wanted most. A "Nook." She is an avid reader and the idea of downloading books onto a device was a perfect fit. She wanted one badly. She had some money. I have enough income that I could have provided the rest. After all, what she wanted was a good thing. We know that kids who like to read do well in school and even college. Reading is positive for her life now but vital for her future. Logic would dictate that I should provide the rest of the money so she could buy the Nook and enjoy the benefits.

But I didn't.

My response of "Wait" seemed illogical.

Instead, I helped her save up her money with each report card and odd job where she earned income. It took all year. Finally, in May, I gave her some money for doing well in school the past year, and she was able to buy the Nook, mostly with her own money.

But why wait? She could have really used the device eight months earlier.

The reason is simply this: Although the Nook was a good purchase, I had a greater lesson in mind. I wanted her to work for something she wanted. I wanted her to learn patience. I wanted her to learn to save money instead of blowing it on little odds and ends.

The Nook was really a by-product of several lessons I wanted her to learn. It was a lesson learned well. Now, when she wants to buy something, I find her searching the Internet for the best price and a company that will give her free shipping. Good life lessons. After all, she won't live with me forever and she needs life skills to survive and thrive in this world. Money management and patience are just a few of them.

Now, consider your life. Consider your needs. You ask God to supply your needs and he promises that he will. But sometimes our needs are secondary to a greater lesson. Maybe there is something under the surface you're not seeing that God wants you to learn as you wait. Sometimes waiting is necessary.

And waiting is always tied to strength.

Consider this:

"But those who wait on the Lord will find <u>new strength.</u> They will soar high on wings like eagles. They will run and not grow weary. They will walk and not faint. (Isaiah 40:31).

Notice what the Scripture says: those who wait on God will find new strength. New strength. Something fresh and vital. If you're like me, you often find yourself in need of new strength. That sounds good, but waiting for it? Not so much.

Waiting Hurts

Waiting feels like you're doing "nothing," but in fact, waiting is hard work. Let's say you have a problem in your marriage. You have studied the Word – you've done everything it says. You're striving to do what is right. You pray about the problem and you pray some more. But the problem doesn't go away.

You may have to wait.

When you wait, it seems as though nothing is happening. You may feel that God is even ignoring you. But hang on a second. Just because you don't *see* God at work in your situation doesn't mean that he isn't working.

Maybe he has to work on something else within you or your spouse before your prayer can be answered. Maybe life-change has to occur. Maybe growth is needed.

See, to assume that God should answer your prayer when you think he should assumes that you know everything. Direct, yes, but true.

But regardless, the truth remains. Waiting makes you stronger; waiting makes you grow.

When the Waiting is for a Lifetime

It's that thing. The thing that never goes away. A physical problem, an emotional problem, a relationship problem – an endless list. But it is that thing you pray about and have been praying about. You know God is God and he can do anything, but he doesn't fix the problem. And so you wait...

Sometimes, though, the waiting is for a lifetime. That is a hard teaching, but it is true. God may not fix your problem and he may require you to wait in life for the final day of deliverance. He doesn't fix everything.

But why? He loves us and cares about us. He is all powerful. Why doesn't he always heal / deliver / "fix" the things that need fixing?

What if the answer is this: God is much more interested in *you* than the *problem*. What if the "wait" makes you a much better person for his Kingdom? What if the problem helps define who you are in life so God can get much glory from you? If this is true, then is the problem worth the glory? A hard question, but one we have to consider.

To put it another way, what if waiting on the problem that may take a lifetime is the best way for you to be everything God wants you to be?

Back to the Garden

So Jesus asked his disciples to stay awake and pray. Something major was about to happen. Jesus would die only a few hours later, but his disciples couldn't see it.

I wonder how often in our own lives Jesus just wants us to wait. To watch. To pray. To stay "awake" in life with him.

How often do we go to sleep? How often do we miss what Jesus is striving to do in our lives in the waiting because we're sleep walking through our difficulties instead of really waking up and "seeing" God at work?

Want to be close to God? You have to stay awake in the waiting. You have to *see* beyond what is in front of you and *see* something greater. That is the very definition of faith.

The Deep

And so I picture myself in the garden with Jesus – him asking me to stay awake and pray. Not knowing what was coming, and not understanding what was happening, but just a person who could see beyond the moment. To have my eyes wide open.

That's the kind of person I want to be.

Com Link

Like many of you, we have a wireless network in our house. What was science fiction only a few years ago is now what most of us consider a requirement for modern day life. If you're anything like us, we use the Internet for everything – surfing, paying bills, downloading music and movies – we even buy our cat food online.

A home network functions on one simple premise. A router connects all of the devices in your home to a modem of some kind (cable, DSL etc.) The only way anything in our home, from computers, iPhones, and even the Wii can get to the Internet is through the router. The router manages all of the traffic so that our devices can access online resources. Effectively, the router is a *com link* – the key to communication with the outside world. Otherwise, our devices would have no way to ever leave the house in terms of communication.

Ironically, this technically advanced system we all take for granted has a mirror reflection in our spiritual lives as well. We call it prayer.

We all need access to God, our Father. The only way we can reach out to him is through Christ. It is through him that we pray. He is the *com link* in our lives to God.

It doesn't take much, though, for something to interfere with our home network. Lots of technical glitches can bring it to a crawl. Like our home network, many things can hinder and even bring our prayer lives to a crawl.

To walk closely with God in our lives, we have to both understand prayer and we have to identify the things that interfere in our relationship with Jesus – and ultimately, our communication link to God.

Jesus, The Mediator

In the Old Testament days, the people prayed to God through a priest, who would also offer burnt sacrifices. Both of these, the priest and the sacrifice, functioned as symbols for Jesus, who was coming.

In terms of the sacrifices, the Bible even says:

"The law is only a shadow of the good things that are coming— not the realities themselves. For this reason it can never, by the same sacrifices repeated endlessly year after year, make perfect those who draw near to worship.

Otherwise, would they not have stopped being offered? For the worshipers would have been cleansed once for all, and would no longer have felt guilty for their sins. But those sacrifices are an annual reminder of sins. It is impossible for the blood of bulls and goats to take away sins." (Hebrews 10: 1-4).

So, the sacrifices were a "type," a symbol, of what was to come – the final sacrifice of Christ himself. For this reason, sins are paid in full by Christ – that's why we don't need to offer sacrifices any longer.

The priest's position was the same. The priest could enter into God's presence in Old Testament times. But now, the Bible tells us that Jesus is our high priest. The Scripture says:

During the days of Jesus' life on earth, he offered up prayers and petitions with fervent cries and tears to the one who could save him from death, and he was heard because of his reverent submission.

Son though he was, he learned obedience from what he suffered and, once made perfect, he became the source of eternal salvation for all who obey him and was designated by God to be high priest... (Hebrews 5: 7-10).

This means that Jesus is the high priest, and there is no need for an earthly priest now.

Bringing all of this together, the concept simply means that Jesus is the final sacrifice for us and the high priest for us. We enter into God's presence through salvation in Jesus, and we pray directly to God through Jesus.

He is the mediator between us and God. There is no middle man – we walk directly with God through Christ, and a primary way we do that is through prayer.

What prayer is.. and isn't

God communicates with us through his Word, through the Holy Spirit, and through prayer. So, prayer is really a com link – a way of communication with God through Christ.

My two daughters talk to me regularly. They have "access" to me day and night because of the relationship that we have. They can talk to me about anything they want because I am their father.

In a similar way, God has given us a way to talk with him day or night, about anything we want, because he is our Father. In fact, the Bible tells us to:

- ➤ Pray without ceasing
- ➤ Pray in thanksgiving
- ➤ Pray for help
- ➤ Pray for forgiveness
- ➤ Pray for others

Among many more. You see, prayer is a way to come before God with our thanksgiving and requests. It's a way to be close to him, a way to talk, a way to be in a relationship.

But there are things that prayer is not. Prayer is not a way to get what you want. Prayer is not a way to smooth things over between you and God. Prayer is not a religious service you perform in order to make God happy.

All of these principles are "religion" based, but God is calling us into a prayer life that is a dynamic relationship. One where we talk with him, find peace, find strength, and often, find understanding for the difficulties and problems in life.

Ceiling Bounce

One day my wife and I got in a heated argument (must have been over something trivial because I don't even remember what it was about at this point). The words ceased, but the smoldering didn't. We sat in the same room, watching TV for the next few hours without speaking. Finally, we worked it out after wasting a bunch of time.

Sound familiar? It's a sort of "elephant in the room" behavior. But we've all been there. Often, we call it "ceiling bounce." You know, when your prayers seem to bounce off the ceiling and never go any higher.

I've been in those times. I've been in places in my life where my prayers sounded sort of like this: "Dear Lord, thank for your blessings. Watch over the kids... and all the children in the world... and... help me have a good day."

Not so dynamic. What does "have a good day" even mean anyway? We can end up in places where we have these sorts of anemic prayers. A place where you aren't even sure if God is listening at all (and you wouldn't blame him if he didn't because you don't have anything to say).

Why does this happen? Often, it's because of the elephant in the room. It's something in your life that you know you need to get real about and talk to God about. Often, it is an issue of forgiveness and repentance that you need to face. Instead, we try to act like it isn't there and dance around the issue – sort of like watching TV in silence.

In life, you're going to sin. You're going to do things that are damaging to your relationship with God – it's the human condition. But in those times, you'll have to own up to your life and seek forgiveness and repentance. It's the only way to break the ceiling bounce.

In the end, your prayer life is like anything else. When God seems far away, always remember that he isn't the one who has moved.

Pray without Ceasing

As believers, the Bible tells us to pray without ceasing (1 Thessalonians 5:17). I think that means we should have a lifestyle of prayer—where there is always an open line to him.

Try getting up in the morning and praying first thing. Praise God for his blessings in your life and make your requests known. But don't say "amen" and go on with your day. Instead, leave things open. As things happen in your day, you can simply say "Thank you for that blessing" or "Father, give me wisdom in the decision I need to make now" and so on. Bring yourself, others, and your life before him constantly. Respond to God's leading and to the Holy Spirit's work in your life.

Prayer, after all, isn't something strange, complicated, and "religious." Prayer is a conversation between a Father and a child.

Sandwich

We were vacationing on Oahu, and had experienced the glitz and glamour (not to mention the exorbitant prices) of Waikiki beach. In the planning stage of the vacation, we booked a boat tour that promised to take us out into the ocean to swim with wild dolphins. Sounded like an amazing experience.

The day finally came and our tour guide, a young, single woman of twenty-five, picked us up at our hotel in Honolulu. The boat dock we would depart from was on the other side of the island, an hour drive. As we rode in the van, we talked to our tour guide, who was more than excited to take us on this dolphin encounter. We learned she had grown up and went to college in Florida, was a marine biologist of sorts, but most enjoyed swimming and exploring the vast underwater world we call the ocean.

After college, she struck out on her own. Traveled to Australia with only a back pack. Eventually she ended up in Oahu as a deckhand on the small tour boat we would take. She lived a very meager life, sharing a small rental home with several other girls. She fished in the ocean for much of her food and grew a small garden. Simple, but happy.

We eventually reached a small port town called Wainiha. A rural, very poor community far from the movie-star attitude of Waikiki. We reached the boat harbor and found ourselves at a very run-down café with a few outdoor restrooms that were badly in need of attention.

After the hour long trek, we all hit the restroom, trying not to touch anything inside because everything was so dirty. Near the entrance of the ladies restroom, sat two dirty children, not much beyond the age of six. The girl held a ragged, filthy doll that had lost all of its hair at some point. After leaving the men's room, I glanced at the children and walked on by.

Back in the van, our tour guide returned and said, "Give me just a minute." She opened a small cooler and pulled out a sandwich, took the sandwich away around the corner of the rest room, and shortly returned. My wife said, "You gave those kids your lunch, didn't you?" The tour guide nodded, not liking the attention placed on her deed, and quickly changed the subject.

I felt like an idiot. I felt worse than an idiot really. Here I am, the pastor of a church, and I walked by those two kids. The tour guide, a young single girl living on a very fixed income in one of the most expensive places you can live, gave them her lunch – something she probably couldn't afford to give. My wallet was lined with vacation money. I could have given them a $20, told them to go get something to eat at the run-down café, and I never would have missed the money. It wouldn't have even been a sacrifice. Instead, I did nothing.

We enjoyed the dolphin tour but that image of those kids didn't leave my mind. I remembered Jesus' stinging words, *"Whatever you did to the least of these, you did to me."* And I… did nothing.

The next day, I was walking with my oldest daughter along the beach and I told her how I felt. She made a simple, but very important statement. She said, "You know, dad, we're just not used to seeing things like that. I didn't know what to do either."

That was true. It wasn't that I didn't care about the kids. But I live in a place where I don't see hungry children hanging around filthy restrooms. The need was there – I just didn't see it in time. I didn't know what to do.

I wonder how often we live this way. I wonder how often someone around us is in need and we're so wrapped up in the "dolphin excursions" of life, that we just don't see it. Sure, you might not have starving children around you, but how often do we simply ignore the person at work or school who is obviously in trouble? How often do we withhold an act of kindness to a stranger, something simple that could have shown them some mercy? How often do we depend on Social Security to help the elderly and disabled when we could get up from our easy chairs and *do* something? If those statements stab you in the heart, I'm right there with you.

The truth is, we are called to be salt and light to the world. We are called to share the good news. We are called to make disciples of people. The family pastor at our church often says, "Sometimes you need to put your Bible in your back pocket and just be someone's friend first." You see, too often, we want to *show* people some salt and light, but we don't want to *be* the salt and light in their lives. That takes work, it takes time, and often, it takes sacrifice.

Yet, if we're going to be close to Jesus, we must have a greater heart of compassion. We must train ourselves to really "see" people around us. After all, in the Bible, we see Jesus time and time again meeting people's physical needs, and ultimately, showing all of us the greatest compassion — a compassion that went all the way to the cross and back.

Maybe that frustration person at work or that difficult neighbor really just needs some live and care—you'll see that if you get beyond the physical exterior.

Maybe that conflict with a loved one in your life is just a mask for hurt.

Maybe your smile and kind word to the cashier at the grocery store is just the thing that will keep that person from giving up.

Will you really strive to "see" the people near you?

And will you offer them... a sandwich?

For Jesus said, *"I tell you the truth, when you refused to help the least of these my brothers and sisters, you were refusing to help me."* (Matthew 25: 45).

Part 4

Deeper

Guilty As Sin

I did it. So have you. It's that thing in your life – that sin – that you never can master. That you can never seem to escape. You've prayed about it. You've repented of it – several times. You committed yourself to walking in holiness with Jesus and to leave the forgiven sin in the past.

But here you are again. You sometimes wonder if this will always be your life. You keep falling down, giving in, repenting with tears, picking yourself up, committing to leave the sin. But then…

Sin. It's the human condition. In the end, we are all guilty as sin. After all, without sin, Jesus would have never had to die for us in the first place. That is the message of the Gospel. You can't even be saved if you first don't realize your condition before God. It is for this reason we need a Savior in the first place.

You know God wants you to walk with him. You know sin hurts that relationship, you personally, and possibly even other relationships in your life. You know that Jesus said "Be holy because I am holy." (see 1 Peter 1: 13-20).

But, how is this even possible? Once we are saved through Christ, we don't become perfect. We still struggle with sin. We still fail – we still fall. How do we walk in a deep relationship with Jesus when we still fall prey to sin and Satan's very effective schemes he places in our lives?

It's a dichotomy. It is mercy infused in an impossible command. It's the face of grace.

Sin and the Righteous

A quick theology review: We are all sinners – unrighteous people. The Bible tells us that no one is righteous (Romans 3:10) and that in our sins, we are eternally dead. In fact, the whole world is in a state of "lostness" before God. That's why the world is in the condition that it is in, that's why everything eventually dies, and that is why life is full of pain and sorrow.

The message of the Bible: Because of God's great love for us, he paid the penalty of sin on the cross and rose victorious over the grave. Now, through his sacrifice, we can have eternal life, which effectively means that we are free from the chains of sin and its ultimate price: eternal death.

This is the breaking point. You see, so many people like the idea of Jesus, and especially, a benevolent God. What they don't like is the Biblical principle of sin and God as the righteous judge of it. Yet, the Bible is very clear that sin will be judged and all people outside of the forgiveness through Christ will spend eternity in a spiritual death called hell. It's a war: the war for the human heart, because we are all guilty as sin.

Once we know Christ, we are forgiven of our sins and made right with God because of the righteousness of Christ. At this point, God wants us to begin living lives that reflect that forgiveness, grace, and righteousness. So, the Bible is full of examples and information about sin – what God labels as sin. For example, the Bible gives us explicit instructions about such things as:

➤ The way we speak
➤ Our general behavior toward others
➤ Selfishness
➤ Sexuality
➤ Mercy toward others
➤ The way we handle anger
➤ The way we respond to enemies

And many more of course. So, as people who have been reborn, the Bible tells us to *"be holy because I am holy."*

But we're still sinners. Saved by grace, not by our works, but then the Bible says, *"Go and sin no more…"* (John 8:11).

But…

But that's not all there is to the story. Even Paul put it this way:

"So the trouble is not with the law, for it is spiritual and good. The trouble is with me, for I am all too human, a slave to sin. I don't really understand myself, for I want to do what is right, but I don't do it. Instead, I do what I hate. But if I know that what I am doing is wrong,

this shows that I agree that the law is good. So I am not the one doing wrong; it is sin living in me that does it.

And I know that nothing good lives in me, that is, in my sinful nature. I want to do what is right, but I can't. I want to do what is good, but I don't. I don't want to do what is wrong, but I do it anyway. But if I do what I don't want to do, I am not really the one doing wrong; it is sin living in me that does it.

I have discovered this principle of life—that when I want to do what is right, I inevitably do what is wrong. I love God's law with all my heart. But there is another power within me that is at war with my mind. This power makes me a slave to the sin that is still within me. Oh, what a miserable person I am! Who will free me from this life that is dominated by sin and death? Thank God! The answer is in Jesus Christ our Lord. So you see how it is: In my mind I really want to obey God's law, but because of my sinful nature I am a slave to sin." (Romans 7: 14-25).

See, it's easy for us to think of this "super Christian" standard. It's easy to think that the great heroes of the Bible had this walk of faith all figured out and they never struggled. But that is just not the reality. Paul struggled with sin just like us. King David had an affair. Moses failed to trust God. The list goes on and on. We're all in the same boat.

But that's just it: Be holy for I am holy – but then there is mercy infused in it.

So…

How do we manage, then? How do we live in such a way that our lives please God, keep us close to him, but knowing that we're people who sin, despite our best efforts?

A sign of a true believer is someone who hates his own sin. Someone who is quick to recognize when he is wrong and quick to repent. In our love relationship with God, he promised to not leave us alone, but to give us the Comforter, the Holy Spirit, who will lead us into truth. In our lives, the Holy Spirit will convict us of sin and show us that we're wrong. If you have that in your life, consider it a great blessing because when you're sinning, God is immediately at work in the power of the Holy Spirit to bring you to repentance.

So, as Christ followers, we live this way: When we sin, we quickly seek God's precious forgiveness and then repent, which means we turn away from the sin. If you sin again, you ask forgiveness and repent – to turn away again.

The mark of a believer is someone who strives to live a Godly life, but who knows that we live in fallen bodies with fallen minds. The mark of a true believer is someone who is quick to ask forgiveness, quick to repent.

… and who is quick to forgive others.

Be led by the Spirit, respond quickly to him, and you'll be close to God.

For Sale

Black Friday has become an insane frenzy in our culture. For most early morning shoppers, it's the thrill of the hunt – to find the bargain of a lifetime. Black Friday "works" because stores offer crazy deals on merchandise – sale prices that are just too tempting. And so, the allure of a great sale price and the thrill of the hunt for that great price drives millions out into the cold November air.

Our economy functions on the idea that something is for sale. Every time you shop, you buy. You buy with a price in mind and you're particularly happy when you get a good deal. This is the way the world works.

Everything, after all, has a price.

But do you?

Can you be bought?
Are you for sale?

Price Tag

Let's think first of all about your value. Your worth. Far too often, we don't grasp the value that we have to God. To God, you are an expensive commodity. Consider what the Scripture says, *"You do not belong to yourself, for God bought you with a high price."* (1 Corinthians 6: 19-20).

Think about it this way: God created the universe in all of its glory. Everything you see around you, he created. From the smallest ant, the tallest mountain, even the air you breathe. All of these things were created, but the Bible tells us that God created man in his image. We don't look like God, because God is a spirit, but we have certain characteristics and qualities that make us compatible with God. We were designed to worship him and be in a relationship with him – a Father and a child.

Because of sin, we are eternally guilty and face an eternal judgment. However, because of God's great love for us, he desires to rescue people from this eternal judgment with a "price." The price for our sin is the blood of Christ.

Imagine it this way: If you had a price tag attached to your sleeve, that price tag would be red and the price would be… priceless.

The Bible says you were bought with a "high" price because the price was the blood of Jesus himself.

This fact should be a great confidence builder for you. The next time Satan tries to tear you down – to make you think you have no value to God, that you're not important, just remember your price tag. Because of God's good pleasure, he bought you with a very high price.

You've already been purchased.

But are you still for sale in the world?

For Sale Signs

You're reading this book because you want to be a person of greater faith. But how do you know if you are still for sale to the world around you? In other words, can you be "bought" away from this path of faith?

As a pastor, I've seen people come and go. People who appeared to be following Jesus – who seemed to want to be people of faith. I've seen them fall away. And there are several common indicators of "for sale" signs in the lives of people who desire faith, but end up following something else:

1. Aside from church, you have little interest in God's Word – unless you're in trouble in your life.
2. Aside from church, you seldom pray – unless you're in trouble in your life.
3. Virtually anything can cause you to miss worship on Sunday.
4. You find yourself at ease with the things of the world (such as the world's viewpoint, sin, world's philosophies, etc.).
5. To most things in life, you apply the "God wants me to be happy" mentality.

All of these are signs of trouble. They show a general lack of commitment to Christ, and in many cases, the commitment is more based on what God can do for you when you need him.

Jesus had a very different perspective. He said:

"Do not love the world or the things in the world. If anyone loves the world, the love of the Father is not in him. For all that is in the world — the desires of the flesh and the desires of the eyes and pride in possessions — is not from the Father but is from the world. (1 John 2: 15-16).

And he said:

"If you want to be my disciple, you must hate everyone else by comparison — your father and mother, wife and children, brothers and sisters — yes, even your own life. Otherwise, you cannot be my disciple." (Luke 14: 26).

See the contrast between the list of "for sale" signs and Jesus' words? They are at extremes because following Jesus is not an easy, feel-good path. Take a look at all of the people who followed God and fulfilled his purpose in the world. They endured other people hating them, they were tested and tried, they were humbled, they were broken-hearted by lost people around them, and they suffered for the name of Jesus.

The difficulty in following Jesus is great. Even he said to "consider the cost." The rewards, of course, are eternal.

Sold Out

The problem with this conversation is we stumble over what it all means. You want to follow Jesus; you want to be a "sold out" believer.

But… you still have to mow the yard, go to work, do the dishes, take care of the kids, school, whatever your daily responsibilities are.

So practically, how does being a sold out believer look? I believe there are four characteristics that a sold out believer daily infuses in life:

1. Humility. You realize who you are. You have a lifestyle based on your relationship with God where you are not proud or arrogant. In that, you're more focused on your relationship with God than on a "religion." Yet, you're not a doormat for the world. Because your life is centered on your relationship with Christ, you are highly influential.
2. Courageous. You're not afraid to be different and to stand up for what you believe in. You are unafraid to really love people, despite the possible hurt. You are not afraid of the "Isaiah response" ("Here am I, send me." See Isaiah 6:7-8).
3. Flashlight oriented. You realize that God has given you circles of influence for an eternal mission. Jesus said, *"You are the light of the world,"* and you intend to be just that.
4. Not religious. You do what you do for the love of a Savior. Not for a religious tradition.

All of these are challenging, but what if we really focused on them and tried? What if we really tried to love the Lord, our God, with all our heart, soul, mind, and strength?

What if we really threw away the "for sale" signs in our lives because we are priceless?

It's the challenge of a lifetime – to be a sold out believer.

It's a different way to live – one the world will not understand.

It is a life of deeper faith.

Desire

What do you want?

Immediately, you thought of some "stuff." A new car, a better house, some new clothes, new shoes for the kids – the list is endless.

But no, what do you really want?

This time, maybe you thought about your relationships. Maybe your kids, if you have them. You want them all to be healthy and happy.

Great, but those things are for them. What do you want for yourself?

Now, you're stumbling for answers, aren't you? Once you remove material possessions or things like a "better job," and once you remove your care and concern for your family and friends, what's left?

What do you want? What do you desire?

It's an important question. It needs an important answer.

What if your heart answer was this: *I want God to be proud of my life.*

Well Done...

As you think about your desire, spend a moment reading this parable Jesus told:

"Again, the Kingdom of Heaven can be illustrated by the story of a man going on a long trip. He called together his servants and entrusted his money to them while he was gone. He gave five bags of silver to one, two bags of silver to another, and one bag of silver to the last—dividing it in proportion to their abilities. He then left on his trip.

The servant who received the five bags of silver began to invest the money and earned five more. The servant with two bags of silver also went to work and earned two more. But the servant who received the one bag of silver dug a hole in the ground and hid the master's money.

After a long time their master returned from his trip and called them to give an account of how they had used his money. The servant to whom he had entrusted the five bags of silver came forward with five more and said, 'Master, you gave me five bags of silver to invest, and I have earned five more.'

The master was full of praise. 'Well done, my good and faithful servant. You have been faithful in handling this small amount, so now I will give you many more responsibilities. Let's celebrate together!'

The servant who had received the two bags of silver came forward and said, 'Master, you gave me two bags of silver to invest, and I have earned two more.'

The master said, 'Well done, my good and faithful servant. You have been faithful in handling this small amount, so now I will give you many more responsibilities. Let's celebrate together!'

Then the servant with the one bag of silver came and said, 'Master, I knew you were a harsh man, harvesting crops you didn't plant and gathering crops you didn't cultivate. I was afraid I would lose your money, so I hid it in the earth. Look, here is your money back.'

But the master replied, 'You wicked and lazy servant! If you knew I harvested crops I didn't plant and gathered crops I didn't cultivate, why didn't you deposit my money in the bank? At least I could have gotten some interest on it.'

Then he ordered, 'Take the money from this servant, and give it to the one with the ten bags of silver. To those who use well what they are given, even more will be given, and they will have an abundance. But from those who do nothing, even what little they have will be taken away. Now throw this useless servant into outer darkness, where there will be weeping and gnashing of teeth.' (Matthew 25: 14-30).

In a nutshell, this parable means that God has given each of us different talents and abilities. We are to use those abilities in our lives. In other words, we are to be faithful by using, for his glory, the things he has entrusted to us.

This is where you have to know yourself and you have to avoid comparing yourself to other people. We are all gifted differently and we all have different roles in the body of Christ (see 1 Corinthians 12). The point of the parable is you use what you have been given for God's glory and for his Kingdom.

But that's where the rubber meets the road so to speak. You won't do whatever it is God wants you to do in the world until you have the *desire* to do so. In the end, you have to take the teaching of God's word and let it change your heart. Your heart, then begins to drive your behavior.

Frozen Chosen

A lot of times, though, we're like the third servant in the parable. We have some gifts and talents, but we don't want to mess up. That's what kept the third servant from doing anything – he didn't want to "lose."

Many times, we might say that we don't know what God wants us to do in the world, but we're also not willing to take risks. You could:

Teach a Bible study – but what if you're a terrible teacher?

Volunteer to help with a ministry at church – but what if you're terrible at it?

Jump out there and try to use your gifts – but what if no one even notices?

The answer to all of these questions is: So what?

What if you try to serve God and things don't go the way you thought?

So what? At least you're putting yourself out there. At least you're moving. You're not the frozen chosen. Get out there. Try something. Find a place to serve.

If you want to walk with God in your life, he will give you something to do along the way. I promise. You've just got to be willing to jump in when God puts the opportunity in front of you.

Fruit

As people, we have a tendency to take an assignment and run with it. You might say, "God wants me to…" and off you go. I'm the same way. As I strive to serve the kingdom, I constantly have to remind myself that "success" is not measured in the way the world measures it, and in the end, success doesn't even depend on me.

When I'm able to "flow" in that line of thinking, which is Biblical, then I feel happy preaching and being the pastor of a church. I feel fulfilled and full of purpose.

When I start depending on myself, I get frustrated. I get stressed. I feel like driving by our church building and throwing some C4 through the window and speeding out of town. When I feel this way, I know I'm trying to work in my own power instead of depending on the power of God working through me.

It's like Jesus said in another parable:

I am the vine; you are the branches. If you remain in me and I in you, you will bear much fruit; apart from me you can do nothing. (John 15:5).

And there it is. Stay close to Jesus. Depend on him and not on yourself. In that, he'll use the gifts he has already given you to accomplish his purpose in the world.

It's really not any more complicated than that. When it's "complicated," you're just making it so.

Back to the Question

And so, we come back to the question we started with.

What do you want?

What is your desire?

To me, I think the most important thing God could ever say to me is, "Well done, my good and faithful servant." That would just be the best thing to ever hear.

And so, I have to have that desire. When I think about the things I want in life, I have to constantly remind myself that I want God to be proud of my life.

The Deep

Because... if that's my desire, then my desire will drive my actions.

How different would our world be if more of us really wanted God to say, "Well done."

Part 5
Coming up for Air

Small Voice

We like explosions. We are sort of wired for them. Think about it – what do you vividly remember? You might say your wedding, the birth of a child, the day you graduated from high school. Big moments. You also vividly remember negative events as well, such as the day you lost someone you love. All of these events, whether positive or negative, are explosive events. They stimulate all of the senses.

Think about it more simply: Why do we like the 4th of July? It's not really the hot dogs or the decorations of the holiday. It's the fireworks. A single spark sails into the air and suddenly (and loudly) produces a dizzying visual array – an explosion of color.

There's nothing wrong with any of this. After all, we're just that way. But what if we expect our relationship with God to be explosive as well? What if we're always seeking mountain moments – places where God really speaks to us in a big way? What if God doesn't speak this way most of the time?

What if he communicates with us in an entirely different way? A still, small voice.

What if we miss him because we're looking for something else?

Elijah

Elijah had a tough job. He had to try to get a group of people to return to God who had decided to worship idols. And we think we have problems.

But God is faithful and he caused a supernatural showdown between Elijah and the prophets of Baal. Everyone was there – everyone saw the fire come down from heaven. It was very dramatic. Fireworks. (see 1 Kings 18: 20-40).

Problem was, this seriously upset Jezebel, and Elijah had to run away into the wilderness just to keep from getting killed. He was so upset about the idea of getting killed that he asked God to just let him die.

This time, God didn't speak in fireworks. Instead, he spoke to Elijah in a still, small voice:

He came to a cave, where he spent the night. But the Lord said to him, "What are you doing here, Elijah?"

Elijah replied, "I have zealously served the Lord God Almighty. But the people of Israel have broken their covenant with you, torn down your altars, and killed every one of your prophets. I am the only one left, and now they are trying to kill me, too."

"Go out and stand before me on the mountain," the Lord told him. And as Elijah stood there, the Lord passed by, and a mighty windstorm

hit the mountain. It was such a terrible blast that the rocks were torn loose, but the Lord was not in the wind.

After the wind there was an earthquake, but the Lord was not in the earthquake. And after the earthquake there was a fire, but the Lord was not in the fire.

And after the fire there was the sound of a gentle whisper. When Elijah heard it, he wrapped his face in his cloak and went out and stood at the entrance of the cave. (1 Kings 19: 9-13).

Many dramatic things had happened. Elijah had seen God work in mighty ways. But in this moment of desperation, where Elijah wants to die, God shows him something different.

A windstorm – but God wasn't in it.

An earthquake – but God wasn't in it.

Fire – but God wasn't in it.

Then, God spoke to Elijah in a small voice – a "gentle whisper."

In our lives, we face times of desperation. In those moments, we want God to respond to us in a big way – a windstorm, an earthquake, fire – that's what we want so that's what we look for. When we really need to hear from God, our desperation to hear from him makes us expect something big.

My experience: That seldom ever happens.

The Track

I was not a pastor by trade. In other words, I didn't get out of college, go to seminary, then end up at a church. I was 37 years old. I already had a "job." I wasn't looking for another one.

But through a series of events and some affirmations from other people, I believed God was calling me to start a church with a friend, Ronny (who would become our family pastor). Two guys and their wives - four people in a very small town — with no resources or funding. It didn't sound like a very good plan to me.

But... I knew I wanted to be faithful. I knew the challenges would be great. I had to know for certain God's will. I wanted an explosion.

What I got was a track. During the summer before our church would open, I started getting up at 4:00 am and going to the track. I was trying to get in better shape, or at least that was my front story. The exercise was good, but I wanted the warm, dark silence of the high school track before daylight in the middle of a Texas summer. Just me. In the dark. At a deserted high school track.

I thought I would have a God moment there. I wanted a God explosion. I wanted a discernible moment where I knew what God was leading me to do. So I would walk the track and pray, and then I would listen in the silence. And I would do it the next day, and the next. I wanted something big — a burning bush, a thundering voice — anything would work.

I didn't get any of those. Instead, I got a small voice. Not even an audible voice, but a leading. A push — a feeling more like a gentle wave. *Start a church*.

The next day, the same thing.

The next week, the same thing.

That wasn't what I wanted, so I thought maybe God wasn't speaking to me about the whole thing. I tried to forget about it. I quit praying about it. I quit going to the track.

Start a church.

No matter what I did, I couldn't get the thought out of my mind.

Flashback two months before: Ronny and I met several times to explore the possibility of starting a church. The decision we came to was simple: it couldn't be done. We didn't have any money and our town was too small to support a new church. The odds of success: zero.

And that was that. We decided not to start the church. That was the beginning of summer.

Flash forward to August.

Start a church.

I couldn't get away from that thought. It was relentless. Quiet. Small. A whisper in my mind. But relentless.

I went by Ronny's house one day and saw him sitting on his front porch. I sat down beside him, and simply said, "I can't get the idea of starting a church out of my mind."

He said, "I can't either."

The church opened two months later. Small town. Zero dollars. Two scared-to-death pastors (not to mention our wives). Failure would be ugly – after all, we weren't missionaries – we had to live here.

Seven years later, we have more resources than we need, a new worship center, and I have seen God do amazing things in the lives of people that have shown up at our church.

But it didn't begin with a bang. No burning bush. No explosion. No windstorm.

It began with a gentle, small voice.

I am so glad I heard it.

Noise

The problem is, a lot of times we don't hear it. I was in a situation where I really had to know what God wanted. I was straining to hear.

But a lot of times I'm not straining to hear. A lot of times I am too busy, too distracted. A lot of times it's, well, it's just too *loud* in my life.

The Deep

One time when my nephew was very young, he was asking my dad an abstract question about trees. My dad said, "You'll have to ask God about that."

My nephew promptly responded, "God's not talking."

Funny... but true of us all.

As a pastor, I hear people say, "I really need to know God's will about a problem, I just don't know what he wants."

It's as if we're saying that God is not talking.

But I don't think that's it.

God is not silent; We are not listening.

In the past, God spoke through prophets, such as Elijah. Then, as the Scripture tells us, he spoke through his Son. Then, he spoke through the apostles as they completed his word.

Today, God speaks through his word and by the Holy Spirit through prayer and our time with him. That gentle voice, that leading in our lives, is often drowned out by the extensive amount of noise we all seem to maintain.

Communication theorists tell us there are two kinds of noise: external and internal. External noise is noise outside of your body, such as a blaring TV or the honk of car horns on the freeway.

Internal noise is noise inside of your mind. Those random conversations with yourself, constant mental distractions, problems, worries, and cares – they are all there, filling up the space. And... Satan loves to interfere with internal noise.

Think about it like this: If Satan can keep you distracted enough to keep you from listening to God in your life, then he knows you won't do anything God might lead you to do.

The noise is real, the distractions are real, and Satan likes to use them.

In our lives, we need the "track." We need time when it's quiet, when no one is going to call. When the TV, iPods, iPhones, etc., etc., are off. We need to pray, we need to listen, we need to hear from him.

The track worked for me – 4 am, no one but me and God. But guess how many of those mornings I really just wanted to go back to sleep?

Satan will try to stop you from hearing – and following. That's what he does. He will fill your life with noise, keep you distracted, and as you try to talk to God, he'll convince you to remain immobile until you see fireworks.

So, you'll have to do the opposite. You'll have to find a quiet time. A place. You'll need to remove the external noise, but even more importantly, you'll need to shut down the internal noise in your mind. You'll need to be in the word, you'll need to pray. And you'll need to be silent before him.

Psalm 46:10 says, "*Be still and know that I am God.*"

He is not silent… we are not listening.

14

Beyond Understanding

One time my youngest daughter and I were building a sandcastle at the beach. There had been a storm recently that washed a lot of debris from a nearby river onto the beach area. Sort of a mess, but it gave us a lot of extras for a creative sandcastle.

As my daughter was gathering up stuff she found, she brought something to me. It was round, about the size of a penny. It seemed to be something natural, but had the feel of plastic. It appeared to have a division line through it, as though you could open it up, but there were no hinges or any way to open it. It sort of looked like some kind of nut or acorn, but it was shaped too perfectly. I didn't know what it was, so I kept it. I still have it – and I still don't know what it is.

My daughter eventually said to me, "I really want to know what this is, don't you?

"Yes," I said, "but I also really like not knowing."

I meet people all of the time who really want to understand God. Who want to understand heaven. Who want to understand the rapture. Who want to understand some things in the Bible that seem impossible to understand.

But the Bible says, *"Have you never heard? Have you never understood? The Lord is the everlasting God, the Creator of all the earth. He never grows weak or weary. No one can measure the depths of his understanding."* (Isaiah 40: 28).

So yes, I want to understand everything. But I've learned that "everything" is beyond my understanding. I've also learned that I like not knowing.

Bigger

So let's establish a principle that you already know in your mind but maybe haven't stopped and pondered in your heart lately.

The principle is this: God is really big.

That's it, that's all there is. He is… big. He is great. And he is good. Here are at least some of the things we know about God:

➤ He has no beginning
➤ He has no end
➤ He is beyond space and time
➤ He is everywhere at once
➤ He is all powerful
➤ He knows everything
➤ He is full of grace and mercy

➤ He is a righteous judge
➤ He made everything from nothing
➤ The cross couldn't stop him and the grave couldn't hold him.

There is nothing to compare him to, there is no way to understand him, there is no explainable reason why he loves us, but he does, and he loves us more than we can understand.

He is bigger.

I could ramble on for another few pages about what he is like, but in the end, you still won't understand him. I don't understand him. Yet, that's the lesson.

A Lesson from a Cat

We have two Sphynx cats. That's the hairless kind. Yes, kind of weird, and yes, they look even weirder. But, they are our pets. We love them and we take care of them.

But let's think about life from their perspective for a moment. They don't work – they don't even clean their own litter box. They don't pay taxes, they don't understand electricity, and they don't understand how the water comes out of the faucet and fills their water bowl. They have no concept of money.

Since they're hairless, they like to snuggle up with blankets, but they don't know what the blankets are or how they are made. They like to be around me and my family. They like to be held. In their own cat-way, they love us. But they don't understand us. They don't understand any of it.

All they know is this: the house is always warm or cool, food is always available, there is always water, there is always a comfortable bed to sleep in, and the humans enjoy their company. The fact that I have a job, buy food, pay for electricity – all of the little ways I take care of them – is beyond their understanding. After all, they're just cats.

But that's the point. They don't need to know and they don't try to know. I never find one of them with a calculator trying to figure out how the economy works. They don't read books to try to understand human behavior. They don't really "do" anything except enjoy what they have been given and our company.

We need to be more like that.

Understanding and Faith

The problem with us: we're not cats and sometimes we just think too much. I'm not advocating "blind religion," for the Bible tells us plainly that we are to be students of his word – we should know what God says and how to apply it to our lives (see 2 Timothy 2:15).

I am, however, advancing the argument that too often we want answers to questions that God has not answered for us. This is the point of tension in our lives: to have faith without having everything figured out.

Yet, we do this often with things around us. If your car breaks down, do you know how to completely tear down the engine and make the repair – in other words, do you really know *everything* about a car? Probably not. Yet, you have enough faith in the car to get behind the wheel.

What about your phone? Do you really understand how a cell phone takes your voice or text messages and sends them wirelessly to another phone, even if that other phone is halfway across the world? Probably not. But that doesn't keep you from using the phone.

We have a certain faith in things around us. We use things all of the time that we don't really understand. So, the concept I'm presenting here isn't anything new or strange. We already put our faith in things we don't understand every day.

In his wisdom, God has determined that we have to be people who live by faith. You know that – that's what this whole book is about.

But here's the clincher: "Faith" and "understanding" are often incompatible. If you understand everything, then where is the faith? Why would you need it?

But you don't understand everything. You can't. The Bible tells us that God's ways are higher than our ways and his thoughts are higher than our thoughts (see Isaiah 55:9).

You can't wrap your mind around him.

You can't figure him out.

He is bigger.

Like a Child

In an effort to make things easier for us to understand, Jesus often taught using examples or stories (called parables). In one instance, he used an example to help us understand something about faith:

One day some parents brought their children to Jesus so he could touch and bless them. But the disciples scolded the parents for bothering him.

When Jesus saw what was happening, he was angry with his disciples. He said to them, "Let the children come to me. Don't stop them! For the Kingdom of God belongs to those who are like these children. I tell you the truth, anyone who doesn't receive the Kingdom of God like a child will never enter it." Then he took the children in his arms and placed his hands on their heads and blessed them. (Mark 10: 13-16).

Think about it – Jesus is saying if you don't have faith like a little child, you can't go to heaven.

But what does he mean? To be saved, you have to believe in someone you've never seen. You have to believe that someone greater loves you with a saving love. You have to have the same kind of faith a child has in a parent. Without that kind of faith, you can't be saved because you can't believe.

To believe… with a child-like faith.

Do you remember the story of Thomas? He was a very faithful disciple of Jesus, but it isn't his faith that people most remember. Rather, he is often nicknamed, "Doubting Thomas." After Jesus rose from the dead, he didn't believe it. He went so far as to say, "Unless I see the nail marks in his hands and put my finger where the nails were, and put my hand into his side, I will not believe it."

Dead… and back from the dead. He just couldn't fathom it.

So when he finally did see the risen Lord, he saw the nail marks and put his finger on them. Jesus told him to stop doubting and believe. And then Jesus said, *"Because you have seen me, you have believed; blessed are those who have not seen and yet have believed."* (see John 20: 24-29).

I love that because he is talking about you and me. Blessed are those who have not seen and yet believed.

You haven't seen him, and you believe – like a child.

And you are blessed.

The Hard Answers

And so, we come to the very hard part of this chapter – the hard part of our faith. What do you do when you need answers from God, but the Bible doesn't tell you? What do you do when your prayer life doesn't reveal the answer?

The hard truth is this: Sometimes, you just can't know the answer.

Consider these:

Question: I have a loved one who died from a terrible disease, even though I asked God over and over for healing. Why?

Answer: The answer is beyond what you can understand.

Question: I waited so long for a child and now that I have one, I am trying to be the very best parent. But, my child has a learning disability. Why does God allow this?

Answer: The answer is beyond what you can understand.

Question: I suffer with depression. I have prayed over and over but God has not taken the problem from me. I could be a much better spouse / parent / employee / friend / servant if I didn't have this problem. It doesn't make any sense! Why won't he heal me?

Answer: The answer is beyond what you can understand.

We don't like those answers. But they are true nonetheless. If you want to be a great person of faith in this journey of life, you must learn that sometimes the answers to the questions you seek are not understandable – not by you at least. God understands everything, but everything isn't revealed to you because "everything" is more than you can handle. That's hard. But it is true.

How do you know that a loved one's death isn't at the perfect time and for the perfect reason in God's eyes? For even God says, "Precious in the eyes of the Lord is the death of his saints." (Psalm 116:15).

The Deep

How do you know that what we label a "learning disability" in the education world isn't exactly what God wants that child to be for a future purpose?

How do you know that a physical or mental illness isn't a way for God to receive great glory from your life? How do you know that God won't use your problem to help people around you for his Kingdom?

These things are beyond what we can understand.

And we need to stop trying to understand them.

We need to be more like a house cat – more like a child.

We need to learn to *enjoy* not knowing.

We need to rest in the fact that God is bigger.

And we need to let the words of Scripture fall often from our lips, "... *for I know the one whom I trust, and I am sure that he is able to guard what I have entrusted to him until the day of his return.*" (2 Timothy 1:12).

Empty

Think about a kitchen sponge. A sponge by nature absorbs water. So, you pick up a dry sponge which doesn't weigh much at all, then you fill it with water and dish soap in order to wash dishes.

But, a sponge has a limit. Once the sponge is saturated with water, it can't take up any more. You'll need to squeeze out the sponge in order to soak more water into it.

We're much the same way – our minds and hearts are virtual sponges. We're always taking things in, but far too often, we don't take things out. There is a saturation point – a limit – where we can't take in more.

We live in a saturated culture. We're bombarded with messages of all kinds every single day. Current research tells us that the average American sees up to 5000 commercials every single day.

Saturation. Full.

And we wonder why God doesn't seem to be at work in our lives.

Be Filled

The Bible gives us some very simple, yet profound, instructions for being filled in our lives. You see, God's purpose isn't for us to have an empty life. God's purpose is for us to be filled, but with a *person*.

"So be careful how you live. Don't live like fools, but like those who are wise. Make the most of every opportunity in these evil days. Don't act thoughtlessly, but understand what the Lord wants you to do. Don't be drunk with wine, because that will ruin your life. <u>Instead be filled with the Holy Spirit</u>, singing psalms and hymns and spiritual songs among yourselves, and making music to the Lord in your hearts. And give thanks for everything to God the Father in the name of our Lord Jesus Christ. (Ephesians 5: 15-20).

Did you catch it? The Bible tells us to avoid living like idiots (my interpretation), but instead, be *filled* with the Holy Spirit. Sometimes we shy away from the idea of the Holy Spirit because we don't understand him. Keep in mind that God is a trinity – three distinct persons who are one and the same God (don't worry, you won't understand the trinity – no one does. The fact that we can't fathom the concept doesn't make it untrue, however). The Holy Spirit isn't a power, a force, an idea – the Holy Spirit is a person – God in us and working through us. When you want to be filled with the Holy Spirit, you want to be filled with God in your life.

But how does that work? Is it some sort of hocus pocus formula? No. Being filled with the Holy Spirit is about emptying your life of the junk in the way of you and God so that he is *more* in your life.

Being filled with the Holy Spirit has a lot to do with surrender. This filling isn't so much of an action on your part, but it is a surrendering of your life to God. As you surrender your control, your heart, and your mind, the Holy Spirit fills you more.

What does this surrender look like? Consider this:

> ➤ You surrender your husband or wife to God instead of claiming "ownership" over he or she. You realize your spouse is a child of God first.
> ➤ You surrender your children to God, realizing that they don't belong to you. They belong to the Lord.
> ➤ You surrender your material possessions by realizing that your "stuff" is temporary and it already belongs to God anyway. After all, no Uhaul ever follows a hearse to a cemetery.
> ➤ You surrender your job, realizing that God gave it to you and you are there to work for Him – not a company. (And you also have to learn that your job isn't who you are – you are bigger than a title at work).
> ➤ You surrender… your life. You realize that your time on earth is very limited and God wants to use you to do great things for his Kingdom – your eternal home.

As you begin surrendering these areas of life to Christ, the Holy Spirit fills in the space you have created. The end result? You live a life of purpose and peace. You are focused on the things that matter. You love others with the love of God.

Being filled with the Holy Spirit is a thing of beauty. It's also not easy.

Breakdown

When we first started Friendship Church, we didn't have much in terms of material possessions – but we also didn't have the people we needed either.

In the early years, I preached every Sunday, prepared all of the media, was the lead singer on the praise team, prepared all of the song tracks, music, and CDs, printed, organized, and managed the children's programs, taught one of the children's programs, managed the money, paid the rent... You get the picture.

It took its toll. I felt like I didn't do anything very well. Sure, the church machine kept running, but so often, I felt like I was running on empty.

Now, we have people that manage our kids programs – I often don't know the details of it. We have a worship leader who manages all of the music and all of the technical details of the worship service. We have sound and media people, lots of gadgets and computers. Honestly, if it was left up to me, I wouldn't even know how to turn on all of the equipment to run a worship service.

We have a financial team that takes care of all the money, bills, and details.

I don't do as much as I once did. I don't know the details of everything going on at our church. But my preaching is better.

I have more insight – I am more creative. Not because I have new skills, but now, I have time to... think. To focus on doing what God has called me to do with the best of my ability. Others are handling different aspects of our ministry using what God has called them to do. It's a beautiful thing—the Body of Christ.

But what if I had held onto all of the details of the children's ministry, or kept control of the worship music and band? What if every decision still had to filter through me? I would be in the same place and the church would suffer.

Now, I'm better at my ministry because I am empty of so many of the responsibilities. I can focus on what God has called me to do.

Greater… by doing less.

Your life is like this, too.

You're busy, yes. You have a lot of responsibility, I know. You do a lot.

But… do you really need to?

Do your kids really need to be in every soccer / basketball / baseball game / dance recital? Maybe they're overfilled with activities.

Do you really need every hobby?

Is every relationship in your life positive?

Do you have to watch TV as much or prowl Facebook as much?

Do you have to do as much at church? Are you trying to do so much at church that you're in the way of other people serving?

Hard questions, but important questions.

You see, it's human nature to want a full life, but we honestly have to stop and look at life sometimes and ask the question, "What am I so full of *doing* that my relationship with Him is suffering?

The Deep

Try this: Take a Saturday. Go nowhere, do nothing. No TV, no phone, no computer, no books. No visitors. No house chores.

Sit in a lawn chair in the yard. Go for a walk. Let your mind question what you're doing in your life. Odds are, with just one day of quiet, the Holy Spirit is going to lead you to reduce some of the "time wasters" and focus on things that really matter.

God will lead you to focus on Him through the Holy Spirit. He will lead you to focus on your faith and your relationship with Him. In turn, you'll be a better spouse, a better parent, a better employee, and a better servant of the Kingdom.

He will lead you to himself.

To be empty.

And then be filled.

Part 6

Breaking the Surface

16

Broken

Think about your living room. You probably have some furniture you find comfortable – maybe it's even new. Maybe you've recently upgraded to a new TV. Perhaps you have a stereo, rugs, nice carpet, pictures on the wall. Maybe some wallpaper or painted drywall – whatever the case may be. You find your living room… comfortable. You like to be there.

Now, change the image. Picture your furniture ripped and torn. Imagine someone poured ammonia all over the floor. The TV doesn't work, there is trash everywhere, and mold is growing up the walls.

Doesn't sound like a good place to live.

But what if that second image is… what's real?

System Failure

When I was in seminary, I lived part time at a very small apartment that looked more like a prison cell than a place to live. I went to school full time and worked full time – busy and often complicated.

A few doors down in the prison-cell apartment, another couple lived. They were in seminary as well and one day they invited my wife and me to drop by. They had moved in not long before and were still in the process of unpacking. On the floor, there was a large box of family photos. The wife remarked, "I know I need to organize those photos and put them in an album, but they're going to burn anyway."

It was a curious statement. It was a statement I never forgot because she was right. She realized early in her life that everything around her was temporary and none of it would last. After all, the Bible teaches that this world is on "system failure," and it has been since sin entered the world in the garden of Eden.

To God, everything around us is in the final throes of death and God promises that, *"the present heavens and earth have been stored up for fire."* (2 Peter 3:7). Everything will be destroyed in the end.

Except us. Except the redeemed.

Think of it this way, Jesus goes all the way to the cross and back for one simple purpose – to bring us out of the death all around us.

Now, if this sounds like a depressing chapter, just hang on. The fact that we all die and everything around us eventually dies isn't new information. You knew that even before you believed.

But what if you really started to see this dying world for what it is? How would that reality change you? How would it change me?

The Power of Temporary

As a believer, one of the hardest things to grasp is the fact that everything is temporary. I know it in my mind, but it is so hard to live out. Everything I own and everything I have only lasts a short amount of time. Even your marriage is "til death do us part."

We see that as a negative. Think about it simply: You get a new car. It's shiny, beautiful, and it has that new car smell. For several years, I wanted a Nissan Pathfinder. I shopped and shopped and eventually talked myself into buying one. And it was so great driving that new SUV off the dealer's parking lot.

But… the new car smell didn't last long. I hit a deer a year later and did nearly ten thousand dollars of damage to the SUV. As I write this, there is a long scratch down the driver's door from a shopping cart mishap, and the sunroof rattles.

It's not new anymore, and I'd really like to buy another "new" one.

But the "new" never lasts. Our houses need repairs, the money gets spent, our kids grow up, and our bodies age. It's all temporary, and frankly, we find that fact depressing.

But what if it isn't? Could it be there is a secret power in the "temporary?"

Jesus gave us this advice: "*That is why I tell you not to worry about everyday life — whether you have enough food and drink, or enough clothes to wear. Isn't life more than food, and your body more than clothing? Look at the birds. They don't plant or harvest or store in barns, for your heavenly Father feeds them. Aren't you far more valuable to him than they are? Can all your worries add a single moment to your life?*

And why worry about your clothing? Look at the lilies of the field how they grow. They don't work or make their clothing, yet Solomon in all his glory was not dressed as beautifully as they are. And if God cares so wonderfully for wildflowers that are here today and thrown into the fire tomorrow, he will certainly care for you. Why do you have so little faith? (Matthew 6: 25-30).

His advice to us about this temporary life? Don't worry about it. I love that. I wish I could live it much easier than I do.

And yet, I have moments of that great faith. I have moments where I don't care about the stuff or the frustrations of the day. I know they are temporary and I need to focus on what really matters. I have those moments.

And I also have those moments where the "temporary" dominates my every thought. We're all that way. It's that struggle of faith. It's the tension of what we see versus what we don't see.

But there's a power there – a power Jesus wants us to live in, and the power is simply this: When we walk by faith and realize that everything is temporary, we have much less stress.

What does Jesus say? *Don't worry.*

Try this exercise: Grab a piece of a paper and a pen and write down everything in your life that frustrates and stresses you. Write down what you worry about. Write down your fears.

If you're honest, that list will be fairly long. Now, get a highlighter and highlight all of the worries, fears, frustrations, and stresses that matter in eternity. Highlight the ones that will last forever.

How many did you highlight? Probably not many, if any at all.

See, the simple reality is most of the stuff we worry about is going to "burn" anyway.

New

So, we understand two basic principles. Everything on earth is passing away (see 1 John 2:17). It's all broken. And, anything "new" we might acquire doesn't stay new for very long because even the "new" stuff in our lives is under the same curse of sin, which ultimately leads to death.

Except one thing: Us.

The Bible tells us we are redeemed and being redeemed for eternity. The Bible teaches that your old body will be made new. That everything will be made right.

I love what Jesus tells us in the book of Revelation, some of his final words to us in the Bible. They are so full of power and so encouraging for our lives now.

He says, "*Look, God's home is now among his people! He will live with them, and they will be his people. God himself will be with them. He will wipe every tear from their eyes, and there will be no more death or sorrow or crying or pain. All these things are gone forever.*" Revelation 21: 3-4.

We don't understand every detail of how the end is going to happen. How we will be transformed for eternity. How God will destroy this world and make it all new again. We don't understand how all of the sorrow and pain in life will be gone forever.

But then, we don't have to. We don't have to understand God to believe. All we really need to know is everything in the here and now is temporary – our future is perfect and eternal.

The key, the fight of faith, is to work each day to live in that beauty – in that freedom. To know this journey of faith will end and our faith will be made perfect when we are in God's presence.

The Deep

To live in a world where we don't belong — to walk as a foreigner on the earth.

That's what we are. We are a people made new who are on our way home.

And that's why Jesus said, *"Don't worry…"*

17

No Weapon

A gun, a knife, a bomb – they all do the same thing. They are designed to injure, and primarily kill. They are all deadly, but all kill in different ways. Of course, that doesn't really matter in the end because dead is... well, dead.

You have an enemy on this journey of faith who works very hard to bring weapons against you. Some of those weapons can kill, many cause harm, but all function with one specific goal in mind for the believer – to derail your relationship with God and take you off the path of faith in your life. Jesus put it this way, *"The thief's purpose is to kill, steal, and destroy. My purpose is to give them a rich and satisfying life."* (John 10:10).

But, faith is stronger than this enemy because the author of our faith is God. I think far too often, we as believers underestimate the effort Satan puts into challenging our relationship with Christ. In the same way, I think far too often we live in a state of defeat because we underestimate the power of God in our lives, too.

Consider this passage of Scripture, one I have grown to love:

"No weapon that is formed against you will prosper. And every tongue that accuses you in judgment you will condemn. This is the heritage of the servants of the Lord, and their vindication is from Me," declares the Lord. (Isaiah 54:17).

This passage from God is full of power. It is a promise. In our manner of speaking, it simply means that nothing is going to stop us and the people who try will be ultimately condemned by God himself. Think about that reality for a moment. You are gifted, empowered, blessed, and led by the Spirit to follow God – to walk with him – to be deep. The promise is already there. We just have to be brave enough to step out in faith.

That, of course, doesn't mean that there won't be any weapons against you (spiritually speaking) and it doesn't mean that people will not come up against you in your life as you seek to follow God.

In fact, we know they will. Just look at the life of Paul in the New Testament. Look at all of the people that tried to stop his mission of starting churches and reaching lost people. Just look at all of the ways Satan tried to discourage him, to take his hope, to steal his joy. Look at all of the things he went through in his life.

But look at the results. Look at all of the churches. Look at all of the people ushered to the foot of the cross by his ministry. Look at how God used him to change the world.

No weapon.

Every "thing" and every person Satan used to try and stop Paul ultimately failed because Paul completed the mission God gave him in his life – a mission led by God himself.

That's how I want to be. I want to reach the end of my life exhausted. I want to reach the end of my life battle-weary, wounded, tattered, and torn. I want my life to matter. I want to fulfill the mission God has for me, no matter what road that mission causes me to travel. That means I have to walk in faith, and in that faith, I have to realize that nothing in this world can keep me from God or keep me from fulfilling his purpose in my life – nothing or no one – except me.

Nothing in life causes us to fail in our walk with God except us. He has given us everything we need, but we have to step beyond the fear. We have to step beyond the mundane: to stop worrying about stuff that isn't going to really matter anyway. We have to step beyond the weapons and the accusations from people around us. We have to spiritually see Satan's attacks for what they are.

We have to remember some promises: *"No weapon formed against you will prosper…"* and *"Nothing can separate us from the love of God in Christ Jesus our Lord."* (Romans 8: 38).

In the good days of life, we have to celebrate and walk in the light of his love. In the bad days of life, we have to remember that he said, *"God causes everything to work together for the good of those who love God and are called according to his purpose for them."* (Romans 8:28).

No weapon.

On this path of faith, we all need a confidence booster from time to time. The good news is God has given us plenty of them in his word – messages from the heart of God to help us on this journey.

The Deep

So, be encouraged. The road is never easy. Even Jesus said the way is narrow. Twists, turns, uneven steps. It's all there.

But as we walk in faith, we have to remember to refuse to walk by sight. We have to depend on God and know that he is always a step ahead of us (and a step beside, and he even steps behind us).

Psalm 3:3 says, *"But you, O Lord, are a shield around me. You are my glory; the one who holds my head high."*

I love that. God isn't only a shield, he is a shield all around me. In other words, he is my front shield, my side shield, and my back shield. He holds my head up. My life isn't dependent on how strong I am, how well I "have it together," or how much I know. I am shielded by the very God who loved me and gave himself for me.

This is your journey. This is your life of faith. This is how you live a deep existence. To trust, believe, and to know that God always has you in his hand.

And so, believer, as you walk, always remember this: *"No weapon formed against you will prosper..."*

18

Paper Thin

It appeared out of the jungle like Godzilla. But it was no over-grown lizard. Instead, it was *Hanakapiai* – a massive three hundred foot waterfall on the Hawaiian island of Kauai.

It all started at 3:00 am. My oldest daughter, then 15, had agreed to let me drag her through the jungle. I had read the hiking guidebooks, Googled pictures on the Internet, and I wanted to see this waterfall. But the beauty wouldn't come easy. The hike to Hanakapiai is four miles there, four miles back, with nothing in between except a red dirt trail, snaking its way along the Na Pali coast, which is the second highest sea cliffs in the world. In other words, four miles of grueling hiking work just to get there, then the same trail back to civilization. It is such a tough hike I even trained for six months before going on vacation.

The Deep

So, we got up at 3 a.m., drove to the trail head on the opposite side of Kauai, took a deep breath, and began the journey just before daybreak.

You start out on a massive incline full of boulders. Basically, you climb over rocks until you reach the first summit on the trail. By the time we reached the first summit, we were already exhausted and muddy – and we had only traveled a quarter of a mile.

That could be enough to make you turn back, but when you reach the first summit, the view is like nothing you've ever seen. Miles of rugged coast line splashed with aqua blue ocean water – amazing. With the beauty before us, we continued on. Red dirt, rocks, up and down the trail as we worked our way along the ridgeline of the sea cliffs.

Two miles in, we hiked down to the valley floor where we reached the Hanakapiai river. This small river flows out onto Hanakapiai beach. Hanakapiai beach is a calm, serene beach sandwiched in an opening in the sea cliffs. It is strikingly beautiful – and very deadly. At the time of the writing, about 100 people have died at this beach, just trying to swim a little. The ocean floor rapidly drops away, causing you to be over your head before you realize it. Once the current pulls out and away from the beach, there is nothing around you but cliffs. No way to get out. Beautiful, but deadly.

The river is only about knee deep, but we had to wade across to continue on the trail to the waterfall. The river has big, slippery rocks and a mild current. Half-way across, my daughter slipped, falling into the water (along with a new iPhone). I helped her out of the river, we ate a snack, rested for a moment, then continued on our way.

The trail turned inland, following the river. Lots of tree roots, lots of mud, lots of climbing up and down. But we had the sun on our backs and an adventure before us – all was great.

And then it started to rain.

And it rained.

Then it rained some more.

My camera backpack is considered "water resistant," but it wasn't resistant enough for this trek. We were soaked, and I lost two camera lenses to water damage in a matter of minutes (meaning this turned out to be a very expensive hike).

The trail, worn down by similar travelers, turned into a small stream of muddy water – as if we were hiking in a creek.

But in true Hawaiian style, the rain didn't last too long and the sun came out again.

After a particularly difficult part of the hike, full of slippery rocks, we rounded a corner, and there it was. Peeking through the tree tops in the distance – a 300 foot waterfall.

With the goal in sight, we doubled our efforts and came to the base of this magnificent waterfall. No one was there but us. There is so much water falling so far that the area sort of has its own air conditioning – its own climate.

After we rested a bit, we noticed a big ledge on the side of a cliff just to the left of the waterfall. Climbable. So off we went for a better view of things.

When we reached the cliff, a shallow cave really, we noticed a small pile of rocks and something that looked like a plastic baggie sticking out from under them. My daughter pulled out the bag and a note was inside. She pulled out a worn piece of paper, protected by the plastic but still stressed by nature. She unfolded the piece of paper and it said:

Brian – welcome to my favorite place in the world. If you're reading this, then you made the hike. I hope you love this place as much as me and I'll see you later this summer.

Thing is, this note had been there a long time. Brian never made it to the waterfall – and Brian never saw the note. We

put it back just the way we found it because you never know –
maybe Brian would show up some day.

We turned our attention back to the waterfall. Pounding
water against lush, green vegetation – glimpses of its own rain-
bow behind it. It's hard to describe the beauty.

It's as though God is reaching through the fabric of time
and space to *us* – of all things. The people he made for himself.
He left us notes along the way – love notes really. You see them
in his word and they are expressed in the lives of his children.
Some people see the notes, realize who they are, receive his
forgiveness and mercy, and are made new. Some never do. It
is the human condition.

But standing on the ledge, looking at the massive waterfall
in a remote valley on the most remote landmass in the world,
I almost felt like God took an extra step just to say, "*Look how
beautiful – and this is nothing compared to what I have planned for
us. Nothing at all.*"

And so, I made a tough journey with my daughter – my
child. We went through the mud together – we walked side-
by-side. She fell down a few times and I helped her up. We
smiled together in the sun and braced against the storm. We
climbed a cliff together – exhausted, battered, and trail-weary.
But it was the hike of a lifetime.

That's what a paper thin life with our Father is like. It's a
life of great depth. It's a journey between a father and a child.
It's a rough and rocky road, full of storms, mud, falling forward, and sunshine.

But it will always take you to a beautiful place.

About The Author

Curt Simmons is the founding and lead pastor of Friendship Church in Saint Jo, Texas. He lives in Saint Jo with his wife, Dawn, and daughters Hannah and Mattie. Watch Curt's messages at friendshipchurchonline.com.

The Deep Resources

What's available online:

Get free small group study guides and companion videos by Curt Simmons.

Watch Curt's *The Deep* message series.

Download *"The Deep"*—an original song by the FC Worship Band.

Have Curt speak at your church or group Bible study, or have Curt lead a workshop at your church.

thedeepbook.net
Subscribe to Curt's blog at curtsimmons.net